ON THE OTHER SIDE OF TERMINAL

TAKE BACK YOUR LIFE FROM CANCER NOW

AN INCREDIBLE HUMAN JOURNEY
OF HOPE

ALLEN CHANKOWSKY

CONTENTS

On the Other Side of TERMINAL

Independently published by Allen Chankowsky. For information about this title or to order other books and/or electronic media, contact the publisher:

Allen Chankowsky
www.OnTheOtherSideofTERMINAL.com
Media@AllenChankowsky.com

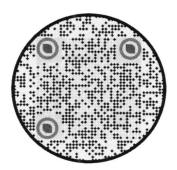

To Ethan and Hila, Mom and Dad, Cynthia, Dr. Madeline Li, and the Princess Margaret Hospital: Each of you contributed to my 5-year survival in a profoundly significant way. I would not be here without you. Thank you.

To my fellow cancer survivors: This book is dedicated to you and your families. Regardless of how poor you perceive your situation to be, this book and my experiences serve as a loud wake-up call to tell you that hope exists until your last breath. New research emerges each day, so keep a watchful and constant eye. Life isn't a practice run, so get out there and live!

About the Author

Allen Chankowsky is a sales promotion marketing expert specializing in contest promotion strategy and execution. 2021 marked his 30-year celebration of surviving two types of cancer, including his stage-4 terminal diagnosis in 2016, where the chances of him surviving five years was less than 20 percent. Against all odds, through Allen's hands-on approach, fuelled by his two children and the love of his life Cynthia, Allen actively researched and managed his cancer, resulting in outliving his prognosis. His personal commitment to himself was that if he  lived past five years, he would write a book about how he became an exceptional survivor by achieving a state of radical remission.

Allen is committed to raising awareness about cancer—and, in particular, rare cancers—through helping other survivors find the strength they need to reclaim their lives. He is a staunch believer that one needs to be in command of their emotional health if one is to carry the burden of their disease in healthy ways.

Born and raised in Montreal, Quebec, Allen currently resides in Toronto, Ontario, Canada. In his spare time, he can be found winning backgammon tournaments at the United States Backgammon Federation, where he won the Intermediate Division at the 2021 US Open.

For more information about Allen and his work, visit his website at AllenChankowsky.com.

LETTER TO THE READER

When I was issued a terminal cancer diagnosis in 2016, I had only a 20 percent chance of surviving five years—and statistically, I wasn't likely to survive more than three. I promised myself then that if I lived past five years, I would write a book to share how I defied my diagnosis.

Well, it's 2022, and as an exceptional cancer survivor, here I am, fulfilling that promise.

I'm an ordinary man with a not-so-ordinary life story. And while I am beyond fortunate to be able to continue adding more experiences to my life each day, I know all too well that the terminal nature of my cancer is likely to take my life at some point: that means I'm living on borrowed time.

But what good is an extraordinary story if it's not captured in some way, preserved so that it doesn't fade into the darkness of time but is a keepsake for those I loved and who loved me back? What good is a story rich with life lessons if those lessons can't be shared with others in hopes of helping them with their own life struggles?

To that end, *On the Other Side of TERMINAL* is an honest retelling of my journey receiving, living with, and ultimately coming to a state of remission after a terminal diagnosis of cancer. It has at times been difficult to write my story, to relive some of these memories. Mine is a harrowing story, which I've supplemented with statistics and research about the collection of diseases we know as cancer—especially rare cancers—and what it means to reach remission.

To my children, Ethan and Hila:

Your arrivals in the world in 2004 and 2007 weren't just blessings; they were the fuel that supercharged and propelled me forward each time life knocked me down. I showed you that getting up is the only way to move forward.

It's not fair that you had to endure my terminal illness this early in your lives. I tried to conceal the impact of my difficulties the best I could and for as long as I could. Every day, I put on my jovial facade so that you wouldn't have to worry about me as I navigated a myriad of emotional and physical struggles. But if I was to get up and move forward with my final struggle, I needed to let you in. This meant exposing you to the harsh reality of my failing health early in your lives.

This book is for you to hold as closely to your hearts as you wish, whenever you wish. When you reach major milestones in your lives or when life inevitably knocks you down, you can always turn to this book, to your own colourful memories, and know that the love and care I offered you when I was alive doesn't end when my life does. Rather, it is my wish that the love, devotion, and support I offered and the lessons I taught through our shared experiences continue and become even more profound as you advance with your own lives.

To the many people who have just met cancer for the first time or are in the midst of treatment and scared about the uncertainty of your future; to those people who are just curious or want to read an interesting story, and to those who, like me, are living on borrowed time:

This is a scary and, for some, paralyzing experience. Cancer appears to have the power to affect your life, the way you live, to whom you gravitate, and from whom you pull away. Cancer seems to take control. I get it. I lived it. I've been there.

What I try to convey in this book is that more people are living longer —and sometimes better—with a disease that sometimes carries with it a terminal diagnosis. If this is you or someone you love, you likely need help and fast. Wherever you find yourself on your cancer journey— whether you are just beginning your battle or are in the darkest midst of the fight and need support; whether you are suffering through treatment or have received news of remission; whether you are the patient or you are watching a loved one fight—this book can help you find the support and positivity you need to get through to the next phase.

I should warn you that what you will find inside these pages is not for the faint of heart—nor will your journey be. But that doesn't mean you can't face it. Taking this journey with me here will better prepare you for what is to come and hopefully lead you to the place that many individuals, including myself, find ourselves in now: a state of remission and newfound appreciation and determination to live the life you want and deserve—a life with continued purpose and profound meaning.

Regardless of the reason you're reading this book, I'm going to assume that you're in need of something that my story offers—whether that's inspiration, basic cancer education, or just curiosity about how the hell I outlived my best-before-date from a rare and notoriously deadly cancer. My goal is to deliver the motivation you need to approach the possibility of cancer remission with confidence and to equip you with information that could help you achieve it. If you feel that I've succeeded, there is only one thing I request in return, and that is to share these messages with others with the view of helping more people live longer and better lives, despite having cancer.

If you have any questions, thoughts, or comments, or if you just want to share your story with me, I would love to hear from you. Feel free to send an email to **survivor@AllenChankowsky.com**.

Even during my own struggles with cancer, there were moments when I felt completely alone and moments when I felt more supported than ever before. I know I would have benefitted from reading an inspirational story similar to the one found in these pages.

I invite you into my personal story of facing and surviving a terminal diagnosis of cancer. Together, we will find solace, support, and everything else you need to hopefully join me and the growing number of people who have battled hard to achieve remission.

Sincerely,
Allen

INTRODUCTION

Cancer has proven to be one of the largest medical strains and challenges in societies worldwide for decades. In 2018, just over 18 million individuals all over the world were diagnosed with cancer. Two years later, in 2020, that number grew to over 19 million.[1]

As the number of individuals diagnosed with cancer continues to rise, the strain of such an illness on our public health resources climbs, as well. In amounts surpassing anything we have seen before, money and medical resources are being used to help treat and find cures for the diseases we call cancer.

In addition to the financial burden cancer has brought on the world, the number of people suffering from mental health issues directly connected to cancer has become an epidemic. A staggering 25 percent of cancer patients have also been diagnosed with mild to severe depression due to their diagnosis—not to mention the multitude of other mental health issues that can come from fighting the disease, in turn making the diagnosis and treatment of cancer more complex than simply healing the physical body.[2]

The statistics surrounding cancer and cancer diagnosis are not all negative in their nature and conclusions. The number of deaths caused by cancer has decreased significantly—albeit slowly—and for many, a cancer diagnosis is no longer the "death sentence" it was once known to be.[3] For many cancers, but not all, this bright light of hope at the end of the tunnel is largely due to the incredible amount of research that has gone into treating and healing the body and mind of the patient.

While, over time, scientists and cancer specialists have improved the way different cancers are treated, there has been little advancement in helping the individual cope with the emotional and personal challenges that such a diagnosis erupts. Children are generally not taught in school how to cope with such devastating news, either for themselves or someone else. Even in our forward-thinking and progressive society, school curricula still do not have modules that teach children the importance of active and open communication when coping with difficult life events, particularly when facing one's own mortality or that of a loved one. Even with school-aged kids suffering the emotional effects during the COVID-19 pandemic, short of locking down our cities, school systems around the world still have not incorporated processes to help their communities and kids cope with the impact of widespread disease and the threat of infection. If kids aren't taught the basic principles of emotional regulation in the age of COVID-19, how can we expect them to properly manage disease later in life?

That's why I wrote this book.

So many individuals do not truly understand what it means for someone to have cancer, let alone how it is caused—nor do they truly understand what it means for someone to be *treated* for cancer, let alone the different kinds of treatments. And too many individuals do not truly understand what it means to be in remission from these diseases, let alone understand the work and drive it takes to get there. For this reason, I have also included chapters that will focus on the details of cancer to help you better understand what is happening to you or to someone you love.

The story's emotional weight naturally calls for some relief and levity. Therefore, I have also included some positive (and, at times, humorous) stories and creative self-reflections. After all, even with a terminal diagnosis, your life does not have to revolve around your illness. In fact, an important part of the journey is realizing there is more to your life—and your person—than the disease you face.

Ultimately, this multifaceted book will encompass much of what you need to help you or your loved one through the unpleasant journey of battling cancer and, hopefully, reaching a state of remission. As a convenience, I've left journal pages at the end of each chapter, so you have space to jot down any thoughts that resonate with you or ideas that come to mind.

And with that, let's begin.

.

CHAPTER 1

HOW I MET CANCER

It was 1991 when I was first introduced to cancer—personally introduced to it, that is. I had heard of cancer before, its power, influence, and strength. Yet I never thought I would come to know cancer so intimately. As many people do, I assumed I would be one of the lucky ones to never personally get to know such an illness. I was wrong.

I was in my third year of a Bachelor of Science degree at Concordia University in Montreal, Quebec, Canada. My life was full of promise. I was studying hard, doing the requisite assignments and lab experiments, and planning for what I would do with my degree once I graduated—aspirations of a career in health sciences. This meant many late nights and long, draining days, so when I began to feel unwell, I really didn't worry about it too much. It took several weeks of worsening health and energy for me to go to the doctor. In fact, it wasn't the loss of energy that pushed me to make the appointment—it was the fact that I had found a small lump above my left clavicle, that space between the collarbone and neck. The lump was, to me, more concerning than my lack of energy.

Although a large part of me thought the lump was nothing to be concerned about, I used it as a justifiable reason to take a break from school that day and do something other than keep my nose in my textbooks. Maybe taking an afternoon off to go to a doctor's appointment would help recharge my emotional and physical batteries.

The appointment was rather routine, but by the end of this day, it would be an appointment that would change my life forever.

My family doctor asked how I had been feeling and if anything in particular had brought me in to see him. I shared my busy schedule, my full days, and my ever-depleting energy, ending with finding the lump above my left collarbone. My doctor shared my apathy for the lump, saying that the chances of it being something more serious was extremely low—especially considering my age and overall physical health. I was only 21, after all.

To be on the safe side, however, and to help ease any worry that was hiding in the back of our minds, he still sent me for some routine tests to confirm his diagnosis (or lack thereof). Even at this point, my worry had yet to increase. I was still grateful for an afternoon filled with anything other than school. The fact that the tests didn't include anything invasive or extensive helped to keep my worry in check. I went for blood work and an x-ray, which were, in a way, relaxing. It wasn't until I was driving back to school that my mood and demeanour changed.

It hadn't been an hour since I had completed the x-ray before my cell phone rang. Usually, I don't pick up my phone while driving, but there was something that day—some sort of emotional force—that compelled me to answer the call. Perhaps it was the fact that no one usually called me during the days, as they knew I would be studying. Perhaps it was my mind having been cleared of academic concerns that day that pushed me to answer the call. No matter the reason, I pulled over and picked up my cell phone.

My stomach immediately sank when I saw the caller ID. It belonged to my doctor's office, which was odd. As far as I knew, doctors didn't call patients to give them news of any kind. I reasoned away my worry, convincing myself it was most likely the receptionist saying I had forgotten something at the office or asking to schedule a follow-up appointment to review the results. The cell phone ringing at that moment turned out to be akin to a death knell; when I answered the call, my doctor himself was on the other end of the line.

My doctor, whom I had just seen that morning, was personally on the phone with me. My stomach sank a little deeper. He said that the radiologist who had examined my x-ray had called him directly and provided him with the results verbally.

In a rather direct manner, my doctor shared the results: the lump that I had found above my collarbone was a swollen lymph node indicating a large mass in my chest. As if my doctor himself didn't want to deliver the news to me, he said that it was the radiologist who indicated that the newly discovered mass in my chest was suggestive of a cancerous tumour. I wasn't sure what was more surprising: the fact that the small lump was only the tip of a large iceberg deep within my body or the nonchalant and matter-of-fact way that my doctor had shared the news with me.

As I remained silent on the phone, unable to come up with questions —or any words, for that matter—my doctor continued. He said that there was still a likelihood that the mass was something much less serious and that I should not worry—although he didn't specify what "less serious" meant. He told me that he would refer me to a surgeon who would biopsy the swollen lymph node to make a final and actual diagnosis. Before ending the call and leaving me alone with myself in my car, he told me not to worry too much and that the appointment details with the surgeon would be given to me at a later date.

I sat in my car for quite some time in total silence before making any sort of movement or sound. Even though it was an introduction that I didn't want because I did not plan to make friends with cancer, a part of me felt slightly cheated. Shouldn't I have had more of a warning? Shouldn't I have had the courtesy of an in-person doctor's visit? Shouldn't I have been given more information? In the silence of my car, my mind began to race, and I was finally able to form words and questions.

I tried to remind myself that the doctor had told me not to worry, but it was of no use. How was I supposed to not worry? I was only 21 years old, with my whole life ahead of me. I had so many plans, so many things I wanted to do, so many things that needed to be put into place that I had not had the chance to decide on.

Suddenly, I was unable to breathe. I began to panic. Was this an anxiety attack, or was this the mass crushing my lungs? I didn't trust the signals my body was giving me anymore. How could it have betrayed me and grown something so potentially dangerous without my knowledge?

I was only 21. I was supposed to be thinking about school and girls and planning my future. I wasn't supposed to be worried about how much time I had left; I wasn't supposed to be worried about something growing and developing in my body that would put a stop to all of that.

I had no idea what I was going to do.

Realizing that nothing was going to happen simply sitting in my car on the side of the road, I took a deep breath and started the car. I had to move; I had to go somewhere—not back to school, that was for sure, but somewhere. Maybe home?

Once I started to move my car back onto the road, trying to focus on driving, my mind wandered to my family; how was I going to tell them?

It must be impossibly difficult and daunting for any 21-year-old to tell their parents that they might have cancer, but the situation in my family was such that the thought of telling seemed like a nightmare that would play out over and over, day after day.

We were all still reeling from the death of my brother in a fatal car accident only three short years earlier in 1988 and the unrelenting shock of our family's loss. Considering whether I should tell my parents about my health crisis, and if so, when, and how, only made me agonize further about the unstoppable pain that my parents were in. How bad would it impact them if I told them? How much more emotional damage was it going to inflict on them?

Understandably, since my brother's death, my parents had become rather overprotective. While I didn't know how the news of my health would precisely affect them, I knew enough to know that it would be impossibly emotional. Not only would I have to deal with my own reality, I would also want to support them. Frankly, I didn't know if I had the emotional wherewithal to take care of my own needs while, at the same time, taking care of theirs.

The passing of my brother changed everything, particularly for my parents. They began to worry much more—or at least much more visibly—than they had in the past. I could see it in their faces and behaviours; there was always a certain level of worry in the back of their minds. To the extent that I could control, I had vowed to never add to their worry or stress. I had been given a front-row seat to the effects of the loss of a child. I promised myself—and, secretly, promised my parents—that I would do everything in my power to live a life they did not have to stress over.

After the news from my doctor, it looked like I would have to break that promise. It was hard enough for me alone to understand and accept the potential diagnosis of cancer, but the compound effect of my potential health situation alongside the loss of my brother effectively paralyzed me in fear: fear for my own future and fear of catapulting my parents into an emotional state for which I deemed recovery impossible. I knew that the loss of another child would surely devastate them.

I was suddenly no longer worried about my own wellbeing; rather, I was conflicted about whether I should tell my parents about my health crisis. After all, I was still living at home with them. Was it better for me not to reveal what was going on? Or was that more of a betrayal because I was not honest with them? The diagnosis of cancer was not yet official, so why would I want to put them through such pain and stress if the mass sitting in my chest was not cancerous? How could I put them through such trauma, only three years after my brother's death, for it to end up being nothing?

The dilemma was gut-wrenching, more so than my potential diagnosis. There were too many variables, too many things I did not know, too many things I did not want to say out loud. Yet, after repeatedly doing the emotional math, I arrived at the same conclusion each time. I needed to figure out what I was dealing with before I told them—before I told anyone. They would, no doubt, have their own questions for me when I shared the news, which I couldn't answer.

Chapter 1 Notes

CHAPTER 2

CLEANING OUT MY CAR

I n film and on television, we often see the somewhat humorous image of characters receiving life-changing news. Rather than do something truly productive, they usually choose to focus on seemingly innocuous or insignificant tasks. I must admit, before being faced with my potential health crisis, I had always found these scenes quite amusing: the stressed-out parent who decides to clean the whole house when they become overwhelmed or too stressed with the burdens of their role; the businessperson who suddenly decides to take hold of their life by becoming incredibly healthy—you know the drill.

When our world begins to crumble and we begin to lose control, we tend to hold on—as tightly as we possibly can—to one small part of our lives that we *can* control. This can manifest in hypervigilance about our diet and exercise, for example, or taking the initiative to clean something to perfection—much cleaner than we would normally.

While this justification for the behaviour seems reasonable to me now, I had yet to fully understand how true and natural such a response to stress is—that is, until that fateful day after meeting with my doctor, who introduced me to my greatest foe for the first time.

Upon hearing the news of my diagnosis, I was supposed to go to my usual class that day. How was I expected to go about my regular day as if nothing had just happened? My mind was full of questions. There was no way I could think about school or anything other than my diagnosis and, specifically, how I would tell my family and friends. This certainly wasn't something you hid from your family, was it? It wasn't something you told someone over the phone, either, right? What exactly was the protocol? How long could I hide this for? Is this something I *wanted* to hide?

I forced myself to remember the last time I was sick. I thought—I *hoped*—that there may be a memory that would give me some sort of clue or guidance for what I should do next. As I flipped through images of my childhood in my mind's eye, only one memory stuck out.

As a young child, I suffered a string of chronic throat infections that resulted in the removal of my tonsils at the age of 12. My parents and family stood by my side and gave me the courage to go through with the surgery. Even when I experienced an abnormal amount of bleeding post-surgery, requiring an emergency procedure and blood transfusion to replace the blood I had lost, my parents gave me the courage I needed to stay calm. I knew my parents to be strong and resilient people—particularly my mother. What they lacked in demonstrable affection and emotionally supportive qualities, they made up for with their emotional fortitude, strong convictions, and drive to succeed in their careers. The invaluable gift of their strength to persevere was instilled in me, and I needed to rely on it at the moment of my diagnosis more than ever.

I wondered what I was so afraid of. My parents could handle the news; they had been so strong for me in the past. They certainly could—and would—be again.

While bombarding myself with my own line of questioning and reminiscence, I found that I had driven myself home only to remain sitting in my car, unable to move. That was when it hit me. The simple solution to all my immediate problems became clear: I should clean out the car—*my* car.

As my body began on autopilot to throw some trash in a plastic garbage bag and wipe down the dashboard and seats, I suddenly felt a wave of calm come over me. Everything was going to be okay. The car was going to be cleaned, and my parents would really appreciate that. If I had to leave, if I passed away, at least my car would be clean; my parents wouldn't have to deal with a messy car. I knew that cleaning my car didn't have to happen at that exact moment; it didn't even need to happen that day. But I didn't know how long I had to live. Did I have a day? Did I have a year? How much time did I have left? At least I would have a clean car—one less thing for my family and me to worry about.

At the time, cleaning my car seemed to be the only thing that made sense to me. It was the only thing I could think of that had a clear outcome. Any piece of trash, no matter how small, left the car; any fleck of dust was wiped away; any stain was washed out. It was a simple and well-defined action with no complicated follow-up questions and no uncertainties. If it didn't belong in the car, it left. If it didn't serve a purpose in the car, it was removed. The goal was clear, and the path to accomplishing that goal was known. Never before in my life had I had, nor appreciated, such clarity in a task.

Now I understand, perhaps more than anyone could understand, those characters in the movies who choose one task and focus on it in times of incredible stress. I no longer find those scenes perplexing in the same way that I used to. Now, I relate to them and find a type of humorous affinity to those characters. I understand their actions; I get it.

Cleaning out my car and the calm it gave me, if only for a moment, helped me digest the news. It was the best (and only) thing I could have done.

Chapter 2 Notes

_____

_____

_____

_____

_____

_____

_____

_____

_____

_____

_____

_____

_____

_____

_____

_____

CHAPTER 3

ALONE IN A CROWD

It wasn't too long after my initial appointment with my family doctor that I was sent for additional tests to learn what exactly was in my chest. The radiology community in the early 90s was not as advanced as it is now. Today, the moment an x-ray is taken, it immediately becomes a digital file ready to be sent anywhere in the world within seconds, but in the 90s, x-rays were still printed on physical film and transported by hand or courier.

Not only was I to undertake the burden of the additional x-rays and blood tests, but I was also given the responsibility of transporting the x-ray film to the surgical consultation. Admittedly, and in hindsight, this task was not difficult or challenging—after all, I was simply bringing images from one building to another, to an appointment that I was headed to, anyway. Yet, in that moment, on that day, the simple responsibility was almost too much to bear. This was no routine urine sample— not only did I have to carry the emotional and physical lump in my chest, but I had to carry the images of it, too. It was the first time my hands physically "touched" the possibility of having cancer. It was surreal.

But there I was, carrying the physical film of my chest x-ray and the results of my blood tests in a large brown envelope with me to the consultation with my surgeon. To the outside world, my package looked like any other large envelope, but I was carrying the largest and heaviest secret of my life. I clutched the envelope tightly as if it was a precious artefact I was hiding from the world.

I moved through the crowds of people, medical test results in hand, feeling simultaneously surrounded by people yet oddly alone. A sea of people streamed and flowed past me, but never had I felt so alone. No one else looked like they had such a secret weighing down on them. Everyone was in their own world, running off to their own appointments, carrying their own bags, yet I was sure—as a naive 21-year-old—that none of them were carrying as heavy a parcel as I was. I was also sure none of them were headed to such a stressful appointment.

The surgeon I was headed to meet for the consultation was meant to assess the viability and necessity of removing the swollen lymph node from above my left clavicle. The assessment was to develop a course of further action to discover the nature of the lump, its connection to the mass in my chest, and its possible impact on my health and life.

The first impression I got from my surgeon instilled a level of confidence in me I'd been lacking since this whole ordeal began. Much of his personality was what you would expect of a person in his position. He was generally a pleasant man who, I could only imagine, would command respect from any of his peers and patients. He also had his many accolades, medical diplomas, and degrees adorning the walls of his office, as you would expect of a person in his position. He was kind in his demeanour but professional and forthcoming, which helped me trust his suggestions and recommendations.

Even before examining me, it seemed like after he scanned the referral note and the x-ray results, he had the singular mission to do what surgeons love to do: cut and remove. As he palpated the swollen node and the surrounding area, my surgeon explained that, while it very well could be cancerous in nature, there was still a chance that it could be something much less life-threatening.

The possibility he talked about the most was sarcoidosis, an inflammatory disease that affects multiple organs in the body but mostly the lungs and lymph glands. He pushed the fact that, in people with sarcoidosis, abnormal masses or nodules consisting of inflamed tissues form in certain organs of the body, ultimately presenting as cancerous lumps when they were not. At the conclusion of the consultation, the surgeon confirmed my earlier prediction and explained that he would need to remove what he believed to be a swollen lymph node and then send it to the hospital's pathology department for analysis.

His alternative explanation for the lump offered me a desperately needed and well-received glimmer of hope. This may not be cancer after all! I may not have to feel alone walking through a sea of people any longer. I could return to being just like them, going about my day-to-day life, blissfully unaware of the trauma cancer could bring.

It was briefly explained to me that during surgery, I would be locally frozen yet fully awake, meaning that, while I would not be able to feel any pain or discomfort, I *would* be able to witness the procedure, essentially watching it be done. At the time, I was unsure how I felt about witnessing my own body being cut into, but I was not in a position to argue or offer an alternative.

Instead, I thanked the surgeon for his time and left the appointment alone and petrified. Although we had a plan in place—and my surgeon's confidence was infectious, to an extent—the unknown I still had to face was frightening.

I'm still unsure how I was able to drive safely and properly, but somehow, after I left my appointment, I made it to my next scheduled class. I was going through the motions of normalcy as if on autopilot. I sat through my entire geology lecture, took notes, and even asked questions after class as if nothing was going on with me. Until there was more to know, this was something that I was going to have to master.

It was at that moment I realized I would need to perfect the art of fitting into the world around me while still carrying with me the physical and emotional weight I had pressing on my chest. If I was able to keep up the appearance that everything was fine and "normal," then I wouldn't feel the stress of having to choose whether or not I should tell my family. Ironically, my parents' repeated conveyance of their "strength, no matter what" approach from my childhood fueled my strategy to cloak the unmistakable emotion of fear and vulnerability I was feeling. I used the very technique they had instilled in me to not show weakness and hide my emotions out of protection for them. And I did it well.

In the days since my initial appointment with my family doctor, I attended most of my university lectures and engaged with my academic peers. But I had avoided almost every member of my family and every friend out of fear that they would find out. I could not have a candid telephone conversation with friends from within my house for fear that one or both of my parents would overhear. The only person that was savvy to my potential health crisis was my girlfriend at the time. Yet even with her, I could not elaborate as much as I wanted to. There was something within me that thought speaking about the possibility of cancer would make it true. As a result, for the most part, I stayed quiet and kept to myself.

I was a man surrounded by people every day, having conventional conversations with my academic peers yet unable to talk about the one thing I wanted to discuss. I was surrounded by people yet unable to make a connection with any of them. I was alone, and I had convinced myself that it would be better that way.

Chapter 3 Notes

_____

_____

_____

_____

_____

_____

_____

_____

_____

_____

_____

_____

_____

_____

CHAPTER 4

UNDERSTANDING CANCER

The word "cancer" has touched the lives of nearly every person in one way or another, either through knowing someone who has received such a diagnosis, suffering from the disease itself, or simply hearing it commonly spoken about in our everyday society. In fact, cancer has become such a common disease that 628 people are diagnosed with some form of cancer every day in Canada alone.[1]

Yet even with its ubiquity and presupposed knowledge of the disease, many individuals still do not fully understand what cancer is. You might be surprised to learn that cancer is not, in fact, one singular illness or disease. Rather, it is a collection of different diseases that come in different types and can affect organs and tissues all over a person's body. Because all these diseases are similar in their characteristics, they are all grouped under the umbrella term of "cancer."

Doctors divide cancer into types based on where it begins. The four main diseases that comprise what we call cancer are:[2]

- *Carcinomas.* A carcinoma begins in the skin or the tissue that covers the surface of internal organs and glands. Carcinomas usually form solid tumours. They are the most common type of cancer. Examples of carcinomas include prostate cancer, breast cancer, lung cancer, and colorectal cancer. Carcinomas can affect any organ in the body.
- *Sarcomas.* A sarcoma begins in the tissues that support and connect the body. A sarcoma can develop in fat, muscles, nerves, tendons, joints, blood vessels, lymph vessels, cartilage, or bone. Like carcinomas, sarcomas can begin anywhere in the body.
- *Leukemias.* Leukemia is a cancer of the blood. It begins when healthy blood cells change and grow uncontrollably. The four main types of leukemia are acute lymphocytic leukemia, chronic lymphocytic leukemia, acute myeloid leukemia, and chronic myeloid leukemia.
- *Lymphomas.* Lymphoma is a cancer that begins in the lymphatic system. The lymphatic system is a network of vessels and glands (known as lymph nodes) that help fight infection. There are two main types of lymphomas: Hodgkin lymphoma and non-Hodgkin lymphoma.

The confusion and lack of education surrounding what we call cancer are not necessarily our fault. Cancer has always carried with it an aspect of mystery for researchers through every stage of its understanding, beginning with its origin. While with some diseases and illnesses, there have been historical texts that can help to trace its origin—where the disease started, how it has developed, and how it was historically treated—there are no such formal documents for cancer.

What makes understanding cancer even more difficult is that many of us are introduced to the disease within the context and confusion of medical jargon. It's only when some of us ask for clarification that the jargon is stripped away and replaced with layperson's terms to help explain what is happening to our bodies.

For this reason, I would like to take some time away—a break, if you will, from the emotional narrative of this book—to formally flesh out what cancer is and what it means to be diagnosed with the illness. I want to release the diagnosis from the medical jargon that often confuses patients and loved ones. Only when we truly understand what cancer is can we appreciate the stories of those who have survived it—and help more sufferers become cancer survivors.

First, it is important to understand that cancer isn't an event. When someone is diagnosed with cancer, it's not that they are suddenly ill. Rather, cancer is a process; when someone is diagnosed, it is because their body has been going through the development of cancer for a while. Furthermore, when someone is diagnosed with cancer, it does not mean that the process has stopped—the doctors have simply found cancer cells in the body, and their goal is to stop the process of more malignant cells from growing and spreading, which can harm the patient's body.

So, what exactly *is* cancer?

Every individual is made up of cells. Healthy cells have a purpose and a job to do; they also have a very limited and programmed life span—some refer to this as "programmed cell death." These cells are created and then die strategically for new cells to be generated and for the body to continue to live and function properly.

Cancerous cells are cells that begin to change and mutate in such a way that they harm the body. Once mutated, these once healthy cells begin to divide at an alarming and uncontrollable rate. They do not have a programmed lifespan as healthy cells do, so when healthy cells die, the cancerous cells begin to take over, multiplying to fill their space by crowding out the healthy cells. Eventually, enough cancerous cells mutate, divide, and take over the healthy cells, forming a cluster, which is usually called a lesion or a tumour.

It is important to note that the cells that have mutated and begun to cluster can be either benign or malignant in nature. Benign cells are usually less dangerous to the body. These cells do not necessarily hurt the body, but they simply do not have anything beneficial to give to the body, as healthy cells do. For this reason, they are called benign—meaning not harmful but not beneficial.

Usually, a benign cluster of cells is removed, and the patient is examined under the close supervision of a doctor to ensure that no additional clusters form. Benign cells *do* have the potential to develop into malignant cancerous cells and lesions. Whether the cluster of cells is benign or cancerous, it is often referred to as a *tumour*.

Malignant (cancerous) tumours are clusters of mutated cells actively working to harm the body; they are those cancerous cells that wreak havoc on the body, either by releasing hormones or simply clustering in a location that inhibits the proper functioning of the body's systems. Generally speaking, if the individual has a malignant collection of cancerous cells, they will not only need surgery to remove them—they will often, but not always, require further forms of treatment to limit any further growth or damage. The goal of treatment is to eliminate any remaining cancer cells too small to be in a visible cluster. We will speak more about cancer treatments later in the book as we continue with my journey.

One last aspect essential to understanding cancer is that there are three general times when cancer cells can be found: early locally advanced, late locally advanced, or fully metastasized.[3]

- *Early locally advanced* refers to cancerous cells that have developed and clustered but have yet to spread to other organs and tissues.
- *Late locally advanced* refers to cancerous cells that have developed, clustered, and begun to spread to nearby tissues; however, the cells have not spread far from the organ where they originated and have not infiltrated other organs.
- *Fully metastasized* refers to cancerous cells that have developed and clustered and have spread to a number of other organs and tissues farther away from the original location in the body.

In summary, cancer is a collection of different diseases caused by the mutation of healthy cells in the body, transforming into cells that actively cause harm. It is in this way that we identify different types of cancers caused by a range of factors.

I didn't know all this when I was 21, anxiously waiting for my surgery. In time, though, this knowledge would come to be at the centre of my life.

Chapter 4 Notes

CHAPTER 5

BECOMING THE PATIENT

When the day of the surgery came, instead of driving to school, I drove myself to the hospital alone and met the surgeon only a few minutes before I was brought into the day surgical suite. The surgeon again displayed a kind, confident disposition and reassured me that it would not take long, that it should be a quick in-and-out procedure. Knowing that my surgeon was so confident calmed my nerves somewhat.

The surgical team asked if I wanted to be wheeled into the operating room on a bed or if I wanted to walk in. Fearing that lying in a bed for my entrance would make me feel too much like a patient, I chose the latter option and walked into the operating room. While my exterior was stoic, internally, I was anxious for what was to come next. Conflicted yet determined to not allow my worry to take over, I hopped up onto the operating table like the healthy, spry young man I knew myself to be. No one but myself would know that I felt uneasy.

Above his surgical mask, I was greeted by the friendly eyes of my surgeon just as one of the scrub nurses hooked up my IV. Everyone in the room, while cordial and friendly, had their heads down, focused on the task at hand. Watching each member of the surgical team and hospital staff move around the operating room was like watching a well-rehearsed play. The conversations were like character dialogue; my surgeon would ask if an item was ready, and the nurses would respond in chorus. Even the lights above me took on the sense and shape of spotlights on a stage, illuminating the main characters: myself and my surgeon.

When I was asked to lie down on my back—a request I happily obliged—I started to feel cold. Perhaps it was the temperature of the room itself; perhaps it was the fact that I had only a hospital robe on; perhaps it was my nerves; or perhaps it was all of the above. No matter the reason, I began to shiver. I cursed my body for betraying the cool, calm exterior I had worked so hard to cultivate.

Shivering, to me, showed weakness. Shivering showed vulnerability. Shivering showed nervousness. It was also the first sign that my body was acting beyond the power and control of my will. It was a foreign feeling, and I didn't like it, not one bit—although I could not ignore how this sensation mirrored the very fact that my body had developed a dangerous illness outside of my control. It was, admittedly, poetic that the moment I finally felt like I was a "patient" in a hospital was a moment that allegorically symbolized the battle going on inside me.

Thankfully, one of the nurses noticed I was shaking and generally uncomfortable, and she subtly gave me a warmed and weighted blanket to help calm my nervous system and steady my quivering. But the blanket did not calm my body entirely.

In a sympathetic gesture, my surgeon asked if I wanted to be injected with some anti-anxiety medication to help calm me for the duration of the procedure. Determined to gain control of my physical body once more and return to my stoic persona, I declined his offer. Unfortunately, I don't think I was too convincing, as he made sure to mention that, if at any point I were to change my mind, he would be able to give me some medication. I assured him that I wouldn't need it as he left my side to further prepare for the procedure.

As soon as he left my side, the lights above my head turned brighter. My eyes were only relieved of the brightness when my surgeon returned, donning full surgical garb, to eclipse some of the light with part of his head. He asked if I was ready to begin, and I nodded in agreement—as if I had another choice in the matter. He also asked if it was okay that two of his medical students observed the procedure as part of their education. Again, I nodded in agreement.

After all of the formalities and introductions were out of the way, the procedure began.

My surgeon narrated every step aloud. It wasn't entirely clear for whom he was sharing the information—me or his students—but I was grateful he did. It allowed me to better understand what was being done to my body.

"I am going to disinfect the area with iodine" was followed by the sensation of cold, iodine-soaked gauze making circular motions over my clavicle.

"I am injecting the area with a localized anaesthetic" was followed by a slight burning sensation, and my collarbone area was frozen. After that, however, I was unable to fully feel any sensation in the upper left part of my body, which meant I had to rely on the words of my surgeon for guidance.

Not too long after, he announced that he had located the lump. It was indeed a swollen lymph node, and it was here that the surgeon changed the trajectory of the procedure. Rather than simply taking a sample, he decided it was best to remove the entire lymph node to send to pathology. I gave my consent.

While the change in the plan was minor, it helped me come to a gross realization. In the operating room, lying on this hospital bed and surgical table, I was no longer just a person. I was someone at the mercy of the illness potentially roaming my body. I was someone whose future depended on the results of a series of medical tests. I was a patient—an identity I had been actively trying to avoid.

Chapter 5 Notes

_____

_____

_____

_____

_____

_____

_____

_____

_____

_____

_____

_____

_____

_____

_____

CHAPTER 6

A SOLITARY TEAR

Suddenly, I felt a tugging pressure in my upper left chest and heard the unmistakable sound of scissors cutting. Within moments, I saw the forceps holding my swollen lymph node in their grasp.

The lymph node did not look like I'd expected. It wasn't as though I had a specific image in mind of what that life-threatening lump would look like, but what I saw surprised me, nonetheless.

It was an oval-shaped structure with a textured exterior, crimson blood dripping from the ends of vessels that had just been severed. The bright lights shone directly on it to make certain I knew what it was; this image would be permanently etched in my mind.

I turned my head as much as I could so that my line of vision fell on my surgeon's face. I was looking, yearning for any clue in his face that could tell me what his impression of my lump was. Holding the suspect specimen in the forceps above my chest, the surgeon looked across to the students who stood on the other side of me and twice, very gently, shook his head from left to right.

I instantly knew that this was not a good sign. The lymph node was not what he was hoping it would be, which had no bearing on what his expectations may have been.

In the world of dramatic fiction, a quintessential image symbolizes the utmost emotional moment: a solitary tear streaming down the face of the main character in times of great happiness, sadness, or distress. For the purposes of dramatic effect, this tear is strategically produced on the big screen or carefully crafted on the writer's page. But it was on this day that I experienced this moment for real.

After witnessing the exchange between the medical professionals hovering above me, I felt a solitary tear emerge from my left eye, rolling slowly down my face toward my left ear. To this day, I am astounded that, in the face of unimaginable fear, my body produced a single, solitary tear out of only one eye. This one tear was pregnant with a wealth of fear. It was the first time I had released—or allowed myself to release—*any* tears for what I was going through.

This solitary tear made the whole experience much more real yet, at the same time, made me feel as though I was in a movie. My life had turned into a movie, a medical drama. I was the main character, and the doctors were scrambling to find out what was wrong with me.

Unaware of the emotional moment he had ignited within me with his simple facial expression, the surgeon placed the specimen in a small jar and continued on with the procedure to close me up.

Soon enough, he announced in a rather jovial tone that the procedure was done. I was sure that his tone was meant to suggest that the mechanics of the surgery had been executed flawlessly, yet I couldn't help but feel a bit hurt that he sounded so chipper after having looked so solemnly at the specimen freshly removed from my body.

I pushed my hurt aside as he sutured me up and dressed the wound with many layers of gauze fastened to my left upper chest. Dressing myself after the procedure, I noticed that the layers of gauze made a large lump under my shirt that I couldn't hide; it was plain to see.

As I was discharged from the hospital and walked to my car, I made the first real decision I had to make regarding the new direction my life had taken. I decided that day I would tell my family everything—everything I'd gone through and everything that had been done to me. After all, it would be hard to hide the lump of gauze under my shirt or explain it away as anything other than what it was, and waiting any longer to tell them would only make it harder.

The solitary tear that escaped my eye during surgery became a sort of sign—a catalyst. I had officially admitted to myself what was going on, and I had officially become a *patient* with a medical emergency. I couldn't *not* tell my parents. I lived with them, I trusted them, and I felt that I had enough information now to bring them into my new world.

I knew I needed all the support I could handle, but the thought of having that conversation with my parents still gave me an outrageous sense of uneasiness. I knew I had to tell them that day, but I still didn't know *how*.

Chapter 6 Notes

CHAPTER 7

DOWNPLAYING FOR DINNER

With every minute, my anxiety grew more and more intense. Five o'clock grew close, and I knew that my next interaction with my parents would be a difficult one. Another profoundly defining moment in our lives was fast approaching, and it was me who was about to trigger it. This night would be different, as would the days ahead of us from here on out—things would never be the same.

Five o'clock turned to 5:45 PM, and soon the clock chimed six. As I waited for my parents to come home, I sat in the kitchen, alone, watching the time pass rather impatiently. While I dreaded this conversation, I simultaneously wanted it to be over.

It was 6:15 when I finally heard the garage door open from directly below the kitchen, signalling that my parents had arrived home. I could hardly hear the drone of the automatic door opener over the sound of my heart racing. I tried to calm myself as best as I could; I needed to be strong and steady if there was any way of getting myself and my parents through this night. But when I heard my parents making their way into the house and up the stairs, I knew that I hadn't calmed myself down enough. In a few moments, I was about to change the trajectory and dynamic of our family. There was no way that I could fully calm myself down from *that*.

We didn't even make it to the routine polite greetings that normally took place at this time every day. As soon as they saw me in the kitchen, they immediately noticed the bulge under my shirt and the surgical dressing that peeked out from my collar. The fact that I had a bandaged wound was one thing, but when added to my body language and the unspoken look on my face, my parents had an instantaneous reaction of concern. The inquisition began.

I had to be strong; I had to show mom and dad (and myself) that I was in control, that I was going to handle whatever diagnosis I was given.

It took every ounce of control in me to detail the events of the previous three weeks. I had to be careful to share only those details I felt were absolutely necessary. I knew I needed to tell them what had been going on, but I didn't want to completely overwhelm them with the details. They didn't need to know *everything* at this point.

Their concern quickly turned to visible dread when I told them I had noticed a lump in my clavicle area. As soon as my parents' body language shifted, I knew the conversation had reached the point of no return. I told them that our family doctor, whom they knew rather well, shared the radiologist's concern: I might have a cancerous tumour in my chest.

At this point, the conversation became excruciatingly uncomfortable. I could tell that my mom and dad were trying to process the bomb I had just dropped on them—to wrap their heads around the fact that the wound they saw was merely the tip of an iceberg that may be manifesting inside of me - both physically and emotionally.

The news was too much for my dad. He quietly excused himself from the kitchen and headed upstairs. My father was not one to express his emotions publicly. I wanted desperately to follow him, to make sure that he was okay, but I knew that I shouldn't. He needed to be alone, and I needed the conversation to continue so that it could be over as soon as possible. So, I turned my focus towards my mother.

My mom was always the parent who attempted to take control of the uncontrollable. She was outwardly unshakable. As much as she was breaking on the inside, she stood firm, offering me her commitment and support that she would do anything and everything in her power to help. No stone would go unturned, no mountain would be too high to climb —Mom would, in her maternal way, do her best to help get me through this awful situation.

Soon after, my father re-emerged from his refuge upstairs, eyes red and face swollen. As much as he wanted to convey strength and support for me and my mom, it was impossible for him to conceal what he just allowed himself to feel upstairs. Most can't even imagine the exquisitely painful moment when a parent first contemplates the possibility that their child may die before them. But for my parents, it didn't stop there because added to those impossible thoughts about me in that moment were the gaping wounds, still fresh from my brother's death just three short years earlier. That my disclosure immediately created an inextricable link to my brother's death is something most people are simply not equipped to process. But my dad knew that he needed to put those feelings aside and re-enter the conversation as a gesture of support for my mom and me. That he was able to contain those emotions is a testament to his ability to selflessly put himself second and be the responsible parent that he is.

I was grateful to have both reactions from my parents. I knew, at that moment, that no matter what I needed—whether it was unwavering support and confidence or emotional solidarity—my parents would do their best to support me.

That night, our scheduled dinner was delayed in favour of continuing the discussion of my lump and some of its implications. The "discussion" took on the form of a question-and-answer session akin to a press conference. My parents would ask their selected questions, and I would answer as best as I could with the limited knowledge I had. I tried to downplay the seriousness of the situation to lessen the stress and worry I was sure they felt.

I told them about the other possible explanations of the mass in my chest—explanations that were much less scary and much more favourable. I continued to say (and would find myself repeating over and over) that we needed to wait for the results of the pathology on the lymph node to be sure—therein hoping my parents might avoid panicking at the prospect of me having cancer.

When dinner finally was set on the table, we all did whatever we could to chew and swallow our food as we had at every dinner before that one. It was of no use, though. The shrieking of emotional pain within the silence was deafening. We could have cut the tension with our butter knives.

The three of us were each caught up in our own thoughts, unable to make genuine eye contact. My parents kept their heads down as they slowly ate. I was unable to eat and simply pushed the food around my plate. I wasn't hungry; my stomach was full of guilt over what I had just done. How was I supposed to eat when I had just sent my parents into such a depressive spiral with my news? Trying not to make the situation worse, I ate a bite of food every now and then only to make myself feel sicker.

Typically, we would have enjoyed lively conversation at dinner. My dad, the quintessential showman, had a unique way of injecting levity into any difficult moment; however, this moment was unlike any other.

An evening in the den watching TV together would typically follow dinner. Our nightly activity of scrolling through the channels to find something to watch together had become a small family tradition that, as I finally realized that night, I had taken for granted for so many years. However, on this night, everything was different. As we tried to go through the motions of a regular family evening, we all knew that our lives might never be "regular" again.

For many years, I felt indifferent to those nights watching television with my family—even found them mundane and boring in many respects. In those years, I did not appreciate the time I was able to enjoy with my family. Even with the history of loss in our family, I was still young enough not to realize that every moment was precious—at least, not until that night. Now, suddenly, I wanted my boring, mundane family life more than anything.

I wanted to protect my parents from any further suffering, yet I'd had no choice but to add to it. I didn't even have the energy or emotional tools to take care of them during this time. I was still digesting the news myself; how was I to make *them* feel better?

While our evening was marred with tension, worry, and fear, we somehow made it through the night. Perhaps it was a sign that we could get through this medical crisis, too. I think that the three of us collectively sighed as the night came to an end.

We ended the evening as we normally did, me saying goodnight to them and heading to the refuge of my room. I watched as they entered their bedroom, as I had done countless times before, but on this night, they were not just entering their bedroom—they were also entering a new, albeit unwanted, chapter of their individual lives and their lives as parents, as well as a new chapter of their marriage.

While they had each other for support, I had to rely on myself. To me, that was what emotional survival was—self-reliance. Who else was there?

Chapter 7 Notes

CHAPTER 8

THE HEAVY NEWS BEARER

The sun rises and sets every day. It follows that same pattern unwaveringly no matter what happens on Earth below it. However, for a time, for my loved ones and me, the sunrise did not bring with it the light of a new day, and the sunset did not project the same beauty it once had. For us, the sun's movements and light seemed to be eclipsed by the tumultuous wait to receive confirmation from my biopsy. Although it only lasted a few days, the wait to find out whether I was going to have a major health crisis at the age of 21 was the longest wait of my life.

The news came from a close cousin, Dr. Mark Miller, a world-renowned infectious disease specialist who just happened to be working at the same hospital in Montreal where the biopsy was done. Mark was friendly with the pathologist on my case. Together, they had an informal discussion, to which I consented, about what the tests had revealed.

Mark carried with him the heavy news of my results as he came to our home as the bearer of the news. My two parents, myself, and my cousin sat in the den—a room that held so many fond memories of family togetherness, many of which Mark had been a part of.

That room also featured a beautifully painted portrait of my deceased brother on one of the walls. The painting, created from a photograph in which he was smiling and wearing a green and white pin-striped button-down shirt, had been there since we moved to that home three years earlier, but I had never gravitated to his smile like I did in that moment. I felt as though my brother's smile was a sign that everything was going to be okay.

While the three of us listened intently, Mark gathered the last bits of courage he needed to share some life-changing news.

He broke the silence to tell us that the final pathology analysis had confirmed the lump was positive for cancer. Specifically, it had tested positive for Hodgkin's disease. Mark explained to us that, falling under the category of lymphoma, Hodgkin's disease was a type of blood cancer. Realizing that we still did not fully understand how such a diagnosis could come from testing such a small piece of my body, Mark continued to explain that the cells associated with this type of cancer—Reed-Stern-berg cells—were found in the lymph node, which was how they were able to draw this definitive conclusion. There was no possibility that this diag-nosis was incorrect.

The news we had dreaded for weeks had finally come, bringing with it immense stress as well as a sense of relief. I had been in a sort of purga-tory for weeks, not knowing whether the lump was cancerous. The results freed me from this position and lifted a huge weight from my psyche. Yet, at the same time, the weight of purgatory was replaced with the weight of knowing that I had cancer.

Again, Mark was able to read the room and sense the tension and confusion as he quickly added that if I had to have cancer, this type was perhaps the *best* one to have. It didn't make us feel any better, but we appreciated the attempt at consolation. While my parents and I didn't quite understand how this cancer was the *good* cancer, we understood the simple notion that it could have been much worse.

After giving us a few moments to digest the news, the conversation naturally turned to the future. I wanted to know what was to come next. I felt as though the only way for me and my parents to fully accept the news of what was going on inside me was to understand what the next phase would be.

I knew my parents had the same questions floating in their minds as I did, as if a dialogue bubble was hanging over our collective heads. How long did I have? Could it be treated? Could it be cured?

Mark began to speak more slowly and deliberately. He wasn't an oncologist. He either didn't know or didn't want to delve into the exact next steps. Choosing his words very carefully, my cousin tried to give us as much information as he could without sharing anything that was incorrect—or worse, accidentally giving us any false hope. He said that my case and results had already been referred to a hematologist/oncologist for ongoing management. I would soon find out how bad the cancer was and what exactly I was in for.

Again, I had to wait for the results from additional tests. I knew that no matter what the oncologist found, things would be different, but I didn't know just how much my life was about to change.

Chapter 8 Notes

CHAPTER 9

HELPLESS WITHOUT A CAUSE

We tend to take our lives for granted. Often, it is only when our lives take a turn for the worst that we seek out answers to explain why things have gone awry. We have a sense of hope that when we find the cause of a misfortune or trauma, it will make things better for us—that we will be able to "fix" it or otherwise remediate the suspected causes to regain normalcy in our lives.

Although I do not fully understand the psychology behind this, I can say for certain that I sought cognitive closure when it came to my first cancer diagnosis. Almost instinctively, after receiving my diagnosis, I began to explore my past in search of an explanation as to why and how this could have happened to me.

The assumption is that many causes of cancer are widely known in our society and in the world of medicine. We are told that x, y, and z are all causes of cancer and that if we steer clear of them, we will likely never develop such a scary illness. Such information is drilled into our minds until we unintentionally believe that, while the cure for cancer has yet to be discovered, the causes of cancer are very well understood. However, through my research in my own search for a cause, I have found that this is not the case. The causes of cancer are just as elusive as the cure.

In fact, physicians and medical experts are usually unable to nail down a specific cause of cancer for any one individual. Often, the cause of any individual's cancer is just a guess, assumption, or estimation based on how the individual has lived their life and their genetic make-up. Armed with this information, I conducted my own research on the probable cause of my cancer. I found, to my unfortunate surprise, that not only are there many causes of cancer but that many of them are outside of our control—and that some of the causes we *can* perhaps control are not as powerful as we may think.

Hereditary Cancer Syndromes

Hereditary cancer syndromes, also called family cancer syndromes, are cancers and cancer-related illnesses brought about through genes that are passed down and inherited. For instance, there are some cancer genes that increase the chances of people developing specific cancers; these are passed down from person to person through DNA.

While there are over 28 known inheritable cancer syndromes, the best-known are types of breast and ovarian cancers, pancreatic cancers, Lynch syndrome, and xeroderma pigmentosa.[1]

It is important to understand that while diseases like breast and ovarian cancers have a genetic element to them, heredity is not an absolute cause of these types of cancers. One's DNA merely increases the chance of an individual developing cancer, therefore underscoring just how complicated understanding the cause of cancer is.

Carcinogens

A carcinogen is any element or substance capable of causing mutations in your cells, thus capable of causing cancer. Some carcinogens (for example, aflatoxins, which are toxic compounds produced by certain moulds found in food) are naturally found in our world, while others (for example, asbestos and tobacco smoke) are human-made.[2]

Carcinogens are commonly understood as causes of cancer that can be avoided because we can choose what we put in our bodies and what we expose ourselves to every day. However, it is harder than we may think to avoid and remove every carcinogenic element from our lives.

Radiation

High-energy particles—such as X-rays, gamma rays, beta rays, and neutrons—can cause cancer in humans, causing mutations in cells. Individuals can be exposed to different types of radiation from a number of sources; for example, living close to or working at high voltage power lines, nuclear energy plants, exposure to X-ray machines, and exposure to atomic weapon manufacture, use, or testing[3] can all be causes of cancer. Individuals are even exposed to smaller and weaker doses of radiation, such as from microwave ovens and even our cell phones. In my case, radiation would eventually go on to play a dramatic role in my cancer journey.

Alcohol

Alcohol is a well-known and established cause of several kinds of cancers, including cancers of the mouth, throat, esophagus, liver, intestine, and, in women, the breast. It is also suspected to play a role in other cancers, such as lung and pancreatic cancer. However, the exact mechanism remains unclear.[4]

Diet

Your diet and the foods you eat can play a large role in the development of cancer. Some types of food, such as processed meat, red meat, and dairy products, have been proven to cause cancer. Eating large amounts of food can cause obesity, which has a considerable association with the development of cancer in its own right.[5]

Obesity

Being overweight or obese is associated with several diseases, including cancer. Obesity is responsible for about 12 percent of the global cancer burden.[6]

Sunlight

Exposure to sunlight has been found to cause cell mutation and ultimately cancer. Sunlight is a major and well-established cause of skin cancer.[7]

Hormones

Hormones are natural substances in the human body, but having too high a level of them can trigger cancers. Sex and growth hormones have been mainly linked to cancers of the breast, prostate, and thyroid.[8]

Immunosuppression

Conditions such as the human immunodeficiency virus (HIV) compromise the immune system, making it difficult for the body to remove mutated cells. When the immune system is not functioning optimally, the condition is described as immunosuppression. Immunosuppression makes it easier for harmful agents like viruses to invade the body, and those agents can also cause cancer.[9]

Age

The older someone is, the higher their risk of getting cancer. Age is significantly linked to developing solid tumours. Scientists think this might be due to the decline of the immune system with age, a condition known as immunosenescence.[10]

Chronic Inflammation

Inflammation is the body's natural response to injury, toxins, or infection. It is your body's way of overcoming attacks and promoting the healing process. However, when the body constantly fights threats, inflammation can become long-lasting, leading to a condition known as chronic inflammation. Chronic inflammation creates an abnormal internal environment that makes it easier for cancers to develop and thrive. Up to 25 percent of cancers are linked to chronic inflammation in some way.[11]

Microorganisms

Microbes, such as certain viruses, bacteria, and parasites, can cause cancer. At least ten microorganisms have been found to cause cancers in humans (including seven viruses, three parasites, and one bacteria). For example, the human papillomavirus (HPV) is linked with genital and anal cancers. Microorganisms are responsible for up to 20 percent of cancers.[12]

We have all heard the story of the person who has never smoked a day in their life but has developed lung cancer. These stories are well-known, yet many of us, myself included, never thought they were truly "real." It was only when I was faced with my own cancer diagnosis that I came to understand. I tried to find the cause of my own cancer, and while my research was plentiful, I came up empty-handed and unsatisfied.

I felt helpless without a cause to pinpoint. I didn't know how I was going to fight this disease if I didn't know what caused it. I didn't know how I was going to fix my life if I didn't know what had caused my situation.

It took me quite a long time (and quite a few struggles) to realize that knowing the cause of my cancer would not provide me with the secrets of how to fight it. Looking to the past for explanation would not give me the strength to fight to live another day.

What I found out then, and what I know now, is that to survive cancer, you don't need to look to the past. Instead, focus on the present and look to the future; only then will you find answers to your questions and the motivation you need to continue.

Chapter 9 Notes

CHAPTER 10

LIFE IMITATING LIFE

The phrase "art imitates life" refers to the tendency of art to reflect what happens in our reality. "Life imitates art," in contrast, refers to when life events mimic images and pieces of artwork. Both of these instances of mimicry can have a lasting and influential effect on one's life. However, what can be perhaps the most bone-tingling and life-altering experience is when the events and details in your personal life mimic and mirror the events happening on a national or global scale: life imitating life.

This is what happened to me when I was faced with my first cancer diagnosis. I was diagnosed in the early 1990s, a decade that represented both times of supposed peace and of great war on the world stage.

First, on August 2nd (my mom's birthday) in 1990, a savage war broke out in the Middle East. The Iraqi Army had invaded and occupied Kuwait in a bloody battle. Such an invasion prompted the rest of the world to react. The Security Council of the United Nations tried for many months to pursue diplomatic solutions in an attempt to facilitate better relations between the countries; however, it was to no avail. Eventually, in early 1991—almost a year after the initial invasion—thanks to a coalition of 35 countries from all over the world and led by the United States, Kuwait was freed from the violent hold of the Iraqi Army.

As I watched this story unfold, I couldn't help but find some disturbing similarities between the situation in Kuwait and what I was going through personally in my own world. The invaders of the Persian Gulf War became the invading cancer cells, trying to take over my body. As I watched the United Coalition put up a strong force to fight against the Iraqi Army, I could feel the healthy cells of my body putting up a similar fight. My United Coalition was made up of the power of modern medicine and cancer treatments, my support system, and, most importantly, my will to live.

While I experienced the war within me as parallel to the Persian Gulf War, I couldn't help but begin to feel a little hopeless. After all, I didn't have a 35-country coalition fighting to save my life from invasive cancer cells. So, I buckled up and began to prepare myself for the long and violent fight that was ahead of me—not unlike what the Kuwaiti population had to go through.

You may be wondering where in this world I found my solace. After all, the Cold War was coming to an end, and my war was just beginning.

Although I did not link this world event so obviously to my own struggles at the time, it turned into one of the most positive influences to help me along my fight and journey.

First, the Cold War was unlike any other in our world's history for several reasons. Rather than being an obviously bloody battle fought in muddy trenches in the rain, it was a quiet battle, a slow-burning war. It stemmed from competition between the two superpowers of the United States and the USSR. Many individuals didn't even realize there was a war going on, as it was almost secretive compared to wars that had come before it.

In a similar way, the cancer had been secretly building and developing within my body. In the past, any time I had been sick, there were obvious symptoms telling me something was wrong. As a result, I was able to fight back—and enlist my troops, as it were—to help fight and win whatever illness or virus was waging war on my body. But the cancer was quiet; it hid in plain sight for many years, fighting a war that I wasn't aware of. In this way, I had my own Cold War being fought within myself.

I quickly realized that I could choose one of two ways to view the battle I had ahead of me. I could either fight to hold off the invaders for as long as I could, or I could fight to not only survive but have a thriving life beyond the illness and the war that was threatening me. It would be a long battle, but it was one that could be won.

Chapter 10 Notes

_____

_____

_____

_____

_____

_____

_____

_____

_____

_____

_____

_____

_____

_____

_____

CHAPTER 11

THE NEXT PHASE

One week after learning I had Hodgkin's disease, I met with the hematologist. From the moment I met him, he made his plan for me and my unwanted companion very clear. He wanted to assess how much cancer was in my body, find the exact location of the tumour, and determine whether there were any more tumours. In other words, his first goal was to figure out the "stage" of the cancer.

I understood this as a series of imaging and diagnostic tests to find out how bad the cancer was and whether I needed to begin counting my days. This staging, to my surprise, was quite invasive and extensive, including CT scans of my abdomen and pelvis, head and neck, and many, many blood tests. You would think all these images of the inside of my body and blood draws would be enough, but they weren't.

The last and perhaps scariest part of the staging process was the bone marrow biopsy. When I first met with the hematologist, he briefly indicated that this test would be required to see if the cancer had infiltrated my bone marrow. If it had, it would affect my body's natural ability to make special types of blood cells that helped my immune system to fight off diseases.

It was this test that I remember most. In fact, this would prove to be the test that would haunt me for the rest of my life—and not because it was one that gave us the most information. That bone marrow biopsy has stuck with me the most, to this day, due to the nature of the test itself; it is different in procedure from all the others.

This was the one and only test performed by my hematologist himself, in his office. To access bone marrow, one must bore deep into the bone with a small, hollow metal shaft connected to a syringe. Medically speaking, the target bone for this type of biopsy is called the posterior iliac crest. In plain language, it is the back of the hip bone, located just above the butt.

With such a description, I wouldn't be surprised if you suddenly felt an uncomfortable twinge; I still feel the phantom touch of the procedure when I talk about it. You would think that a procedure such as this would be performed in an operating room under a general anaesthetic— that would be the most comfortable option, surely. Unfortunately, the procedure is usually done by a hematologist/oncologist in their clinic exam room with only local skin freezing. For a comparison, think of something akin to a dental freezing.

As I lay in his office, my skin fully frozen, the doctor began the process of inserting the hollowed metal boring shaft into my bone with a twisting motion, such that the sharp teeth at the end of the metal shaft would shred downward into the target bone.

At that moment, I felt two immense pressures. The first was the mental pressure and emotional weight of what I was going through personally and medically; the second was the mirrored physical pressure of the doctor, a large-framed man, putting his entire weight into the downward motion. With the examination table paper crinkling with every movement, the combined pressures pushed my entire body into the examination table. I tried my hardest to fight the weight and pressure, not to allow them to completely crush my body or my spirit. I could feel my body fighting back against the weight of the doctor on my back and the weight of my cancer on my mind. I feared I would not be able to withstand the stress of both for much longer.

Fortunately, the physical pressure in my back and hips was alleviated, if only slightly, when my doctor attached a syringe and pulled back on the plunger to create a negative pressure suction effect, which was to extract the marrow into the syringe for analysis.

I was still in my own head, trying to resist the emotional pressure, when my doctor startled me, telling me that the procedure was done and that the marrow had been successfully extracted. He had been talking with me throughout the entire procedure, both in idle chatter as he had been trained to do in medical school and by letting me know what he was doing to my body. However, it was clear to me that, to my surprise, I hadn't been listening to him. I had been able to carry on an entire conversation with him without being fully conscious of doing so.

Suddenly, fear washed over me. What if that was what I was going to have to do until this was all over? What if I had to simply go through the motions? What if I had to move through my life in a state of semi-consciousness? Was that really a healthy way of living? I was sure that it was not. With this realization, I forced myself to be fully present, physically and emotionally, for the rest of the appointment, even if it was almost over. My efforts were thwarted when I saw what the doctor held in his hands.

I watched in surreal fear as the doctor placed the bone marrow into a jar containing a special preservative. The bone marrow itself had the appearance of a miniature red-and-white-striped candy cane. I experienced cognitive dissonance, as I couldn't fathom that this "thing" had just come from my body. Was this the foretelling of what was to come? Was I going to be reduced to being a "thing" in the medical system?

This was no ordinary medical sample like one is accustomed to producing (such as a urine sample). What surprised me the most was that my doctor nonchalantly placed the jar on his desk, as if it were any other everyday object, and proceeded to tell me that the wound would take a few days to heal, instructing me to rest up and take Tylenol or Advil if the pain was intolerable. I had just gone through an entire existential monologue in my mind during the procedure, in addition to the out-of-body experience I was having looking at the jar on his desk, and all he could say was the basic medical after-care instructions for my wound.

That night, with the wound bandaged, it throbbed with a dull, aching pain. It wasn't intolerable, but it was an undeniably constant reminder of what had happened a few hours earlier in the hemeatologist's office.

On this night—as I tried to rest my body and mind, to think about what the results of my test would show—I came to the realization that this battle was one for my mind as much as for my body.

Chapter 11 Notes

_____

_____

_____

_____

_____

_____

_____

_____

_____

_____

_____

_____

_____

_____

CHAPTER 12

UNDERSTANDING CANCER STAGING

Staging is a process that tells medical professionals and the patient how far cancer has spread throughout the body and how severe it is. At this point, it would be wise to discuss cancer staging and classification systems.

According to the Canadian Cancer Society, staging classifies cancers based on how much cancer is in the body—that is, how many tumours and how large—and the location of the cancer where it was first found. Just as we use the singular term "cancer" to denote a collection of illnesses, we use the term "staging" to denote a collection of classification systems. This is because different staging systems are employed for different types and forms of cancer.[1]

The staging system used most often in Canada is referred to as the TNM system. This staging system is used specifically to stage solid tumours, such as salivary gland cancers, breast cancers, prostate cancers, and other lumps and tumours that form within the body.

TNM is an acronym for how the staging system works to classify the different stages of cancer.

- *The "T" stands for "tumour."* In this part of the staging process, the size of the first or primary tumour is described. This description includes how large the tumour has grown— if an initial size was taken previously—and if the tumour has spread to other parts of the initial organ or body. "T" is conventionally given as a numerical score from 1–4. A higher score indicates that the tumour is larger and has grown into another area of the body.
- *The "N" stands for "node" or "lymph node."* This part of the staging process determines whether the cancer has infiltrated the lymph nodes around the organ. "N" is given as a number from 0–3. Zero means that the cancer has not spread to any surrounding lymph nodes, while a number from 1-3 means that it has. Again, the number increases with the severity of the cancer's spread.
- *The "M" stands for "metastasis."* This part of the staging process determines whether the cancer has spread to other parts of the body by way of the blood and circulatory system. Again, it is represented by the letter "M" followed by a number from 0–1. Zero means the cancer has not metastasized, while 1 means it has.

All these categories are taken into consideration, and then doctors assign the cancer a stage overall that ranges from 0–4. The higher the number, the more severe the cancer. At times, there may be lowercase letters after the staging to denote further information about the type of cancer.

For most types of cancer, the stages mean the following:

- *Stage 0:* Known as *carcinoma in situ*, or cancer "in place," this cancer has not grown large or spread outside of the initial tissue; to some, this is called a *precancerous* stage.
- *Stage 1:* The tumour is generally on the small side, and it has yet to grow outside of the tissue it originated in.
- *Stages 2 and 3:* The tumour is on the larger side or has grown outside of the organ and tissue it originated in.
- *Stage 4:* The cancer has spread through the blood to another part of the body.

Interestingly—and importantly—once a stage has been decided on, it does not change. If the cancer changes in any way, it keeps its initial staging, and additional details are added to it. For example, if a stage 2 cancer comes back, recurring after it was initially treated, it is still stage 2 cancer —however, it is called a stage 2 cancer that has recurred. Alternatively, if the cancer has spread to another part of the body after treatment, it is still stage 2 cancer, but it is metastatic. This is important because research and statistics about survival rates are based on the initial staging information.

In my case, since Hodgkin's disease falls under the umbrella of lymphoma, the staging system used is different from the solid tumour staging classification system discussed above.

The staging system for lymphomas has gone through several refinements over the past 71 years. In 1950, the very first lymphoma classification system was referred to as the Peters classification system.[2] In 1965, after a series of evaluations, refinements, and developments, the Peters classification system was updated to the Rye classification system.[3] Then, in the 1970s, experts from the United States, United Kingdom, Germany, and France formed a committee on Hodgkin's disease staging classification. This committee was held in Ann Arbor, Michigan, where they updated the Rye system with more current medical information and renamed it the Ann Arbor staging system.[4]

In 1988, another group of experts and medical professionals met in Cotswold, England, and updated the Ann Arbor classification system to the Cotswold classification system.[5] Most recently, in June of 2011, a much more extensive team of cancer experts from around the world met at a workshop at the 11th International Conference on Malignant Lymphoma (ICML) in Lugano, Switzerland, to update and further refine the lymphoma classification system with yet more detailed medical and imaging information. After a series of meetings and conference calls, a subsequent workshop was held at the 12th ICML in Lugano, Switzerland, in 2013. The result of those meetings was the new Lugano classification, which is the current lymphoma staging classification used today. [6]

It may seem a little extensive to have so many revisions to the staging systems for lymphomas and blood-based cancers. However, as these cancers present themselves in more complex ways than their solid tumour counterparts, continuous revisions of the classification system are needed to ensure standard staging approaches are kept current with technological and medical advancements.

Doctors use well-defined criteria to identify the stage of Hodgkin's disease at diagnosis. While I won't discuss all those criteria in this book, I will refer to my Hodgkin's disease as being designated stage 2A (IIA). According to Cancer Research UK, stage 2A (IIA) Hodgkin's lymphoma refers to cancer affecting two or more groups of lymph nodes located on one side (either above or below) the diaphragm, and/or the cancer is in an extranodal site, as discussed below.[7]

Another important feature of the lymphoma staging classification system is the assignment of letters after the number. The letter "A" refers to cancer in which the patient is asymptomatic. When patients experience Hodgkin's disease symptoms—including heavy sweating at night, high temperatures that come and go, often at night, and unexplained weight loss (more than a tenth of your body weight in six months)—these are referred to as "B" symptoms. So if a patient has any or all of these symptoms at the time of diagnosis, their stage would be followed by the letter "B."

Regardless of the stage, there may also be a designation of "bulky" given to the disease, which means that either the patient has a lymph node 10cm or more in size, or the disease is located in the centre of their chest and is at least a third of the width of their chest. Doctors look at whether the lymphoma is affecting the lymph nodes and organs of the lymphatic system, called lymphatic sites, or areas outside of the lymphatic sites, called extranodal (or extralymphatic) sites. Lymphatic sites may include a group of lymph nodes or an organ of the lymphatic system, such as the thymus or spleen, and as discussed earlier, extranodal sites include the lungs, liver, bone marrow, kidneys, brain, spinal cord, and other organs. Doctors may also use the letter "E" after the stage number if a patient has lymphoma outside of the lymphatic system.

Essentially, the staging system of cancer is a delicate, complicated, and incredibly important process. Without it, selecting the most appropriate treatment approach would be nearly impossible. I didn't know until much later how the stage of my cancer affected my motivation to fight it and to find my own treatment methods to do so.

Chapter 12 Notes

_____

_____

_____

_____

_____

_____

_____

_____

_____

_____

_____

_____

_____

_____

_____

_____

CHAPTER 13

MY TREATMENT CHOICE AND MOTIVATION

Once all the tests had been completed, I waited to receive my official staging. I was half-expecting some kind of cancer membership card. I mean, what better way to join a club if not by having your own personalized membership card to carry around?

It appeared as though the wait for my results would never end. The time passed, and I simply lay in wait while the world happened around me. I felt like a dog that was told to stop, sit, and stay, awaiting further instructions.

Finally, after an uncomfortable amount of waiting, the results of my cancer staging came in. As discussed earlier, my Hodgkin's disease was designated as stage 2A. While I did not have any "B" symptoms, I did have bulky disease in the middle of my chest—or, in medical terms, my mediastinum. With the results in, the next step was to consider treatment options.

This staging brought with it a sense of hope—along with an entire cancer care team. The team met together in a sort of conference soon after my staging results were revealed to figure out the best treatment approach.

When it came to my specific cancer, there was some debate as to which treatment method would be best to target my disease and give me the highest chances of survival. The health team (called a tumour board) was initially conflicted between those who favoured one treatment method over another. Part of my medical care team thought it would be best for me to receive chemotherapy followed by radiation, while other cancer experts on the tumour board thought that radiation therapy alone would be the best approach.

Many favoured the latter approach of radiation delivered alone for a few reasons: first, because radiation alone had the fewest immediate side effects, and second—and perhaps more importantly—a growing body of evidence at the time suggested that stage 2A Hodgkin's disease responded well to radiation alone, even with bulky disease like mine.

After much deliberation, my team decided that eight weeks of radiation therapy alone would be the best treatment option to address my disease. To make the eight weeks of radiation treatment less daunting, the treatment was to be broken up into two four-week sessions of radiation treatment, each delivered to different parts of my upper body. The first four weeks were to be "mantle field radiation," which would be followed by four weeks of "para-aortic field radiation."

They explained to me that mantle field radiation—which was discovered in the 1960s and stayed popular through the 1990s—is a type of radiation treatment used most often and specifically for Hodgkin's lymphoma. It was found to help boost the cure rates of Hodgkin's lymphoma when the radiation was specifically targeted to a large area of the neck, chest, and armpits. This type of radiation treatment received its name based on where the radiation was to be targeted, namely in the larger upper body areas.

Etymologically speaking, I was told that its name was rooted in the word for a piece of clothing: *mantellum* is the Latin word for a type of cloak, a garment that covers the shoulders, chest, and neck of the wearer. While this cape-type cloak was popular from the 12th to the 16th centuries, it eventually came to lend its name to the area where radiation treatment would be directed.[1]

By the time I had received my mantle field radiation treatment, there had been quite a few advancements and modifications made to the method since it was first used. Initially, the radiation field of this treatment affected some rather delicate organs, such as the lungs and the heart. Therefore, heavy lead shields were developed to block these more susceptible organs from the radiation, thereby lessening the chances of dangerous side effects. In short, by the time the treatment was used on me, many members of my medical care team were confident that it would treat my cancer successfully.

However, mantle field radiation was not my only course of radiation treatment. The following four weeks would be filled with para-aortic field radiation treatment. This type of radiation is similar to the first, as it is delivered to one specific part of the body—but this time, it was directed to the lower part of the chest and the abdominal area, targeting cancer that may have migrated there.

This course of treatment did, however, trigger a cascade of sessions with a number of highly specialized radiation oncology planning technicians. While the debate was over among the professionals on my team, it persisted for me because I wasn't totally convinced that the radiation-only approach was the correct choice. My research at the time suggested that chemotherapy was most definitely a viable option for my stage of disease.

I yearned to have the authority and knowledge to share my *own* opinion about my treatment. I wanted so badly to be able to make an educated choice for myself rather than simply listening to what my medical team was suggesting. I was already feeling helpless as a patient and sufferer of cancer; I did not want to be at the mercy of those who knew more than me, too. I didn't have a say in my body developing cancer, but I wanted a say in how my body was going to fight it.

I was not a cancer specialist and had zero experience that would support my preferred treatment approach. However, I was the President and CEO of my body. Above anyone else, I felt that after appropriate consultations, I had the moral, legal and ethical obligation to decide what happens next.

After my team's choice to pursue radiation treatment—a choice that I would later wish I had challenged more—I decided to begin doing research for myself. I wanted to understand what was going on inside my body, both with the illness and the treatments. I wanted to know as much as I could about those who had the unfortunate experience of navigating this process before me.

During my research, I came across a book from Dr. Mortimer J. Lacher and Dr. John R. Redman entitled *Hodgkin's Disease: The Consequences of Survival*. I found the title intriguing and foretelling. The major theme of these doctors' work revolved around the long-term effects of surviving Hodgkin's disease.

Reading the book etched a permanent mark on my brain because I so desperately wanted to be a long-term survivor—and, if I was lucky enough to become one, I needed to be prepared for the possible consequences. I was elated to find a book about the disease I needed to fight. That people—smart people—took the time to write about how patients survive Hodgkin's disease provided me with a certain measure of relief from the anxiety of an early death.

But that relief was short-lived; the book was certain to qualify that, if I were to survive, there was to be a quid pro quo of sorts—mine would be a consequential survival. While it was clear that these treatment consequences would be way down the road and not immediate, it still never sat well with me. Nevertheless, I had a goal that needed to be achieved: survival, at any cost, no matter how far down the road these consequences may ensue.

Survival is such an innate feature of life, no matter the species and no matter the foe. The cancer inside me had the same goal as I did, but I was steadfast in my resolve to outlive Hodgkin's disease. The will to live—not to die so early in life—was too strong for me to be weighed down by the possible consequences of survival. While I was just outside of my teenage-hood, the stubbornness of my youth persisted, and I was more determined to live than at any point in my short life.

For my own sake, I needed to know what was coming next. It was this research that pushed me forward during the first phase of my cancer treatments. It was in this research that I first found my motivation. I took this newfound knowledge and turned it into the power to fight in my quest to survive.

Chapter 13 Notes

CHAPTER 14

UNDERSTANDING CANCER TREATMENTS

B efore we delve into the various treatments, I feel compelled to highlight an exceptionally important (and not well-publicized) development in the world of cancer care.

The management of cancer over the past 100 years in industrialized societies dictates an expected number of cancer cases per year. These cases are tracked as they are discovered and reported. Cancer is often first found in routine screenings of asymptomatic people, as well as when people attend a health care setting to address symptoms relating to their soon-to-be diagnosed cancer. Sometimes cancer is an incidental finding when screening for other health conditions. After diagnosis, cases usually progress to staging and then to surgery, treatment, or both.

This pattern of case management is perennially dependable—and for good reason. Governments organize their annual cancer care budgets, research efforts, and human resources accordingly to help manage the expected case counts. However, as of March 2020, something interrupted this expected pattern in a way that seemed to drive down the number of new cancer cases otherwise expected to occur.

The phenomenon in question is that global lockdowns during the

COVID-19 pandemic prevented people from receiving routine cancer screenings. Many hospital departments were forced to close, and scheduled appointments and surgeries were postponed, delayed, or outright cancelled. In addition, many who developed cancer symptoms were either too scared to attend a hospital setting due to fear of contracting COVID-19 or were otherwise not sufficiently motivated to seek assessment for reasons related to the pandemic. Either way, the fact that so many people delayed or were forced to delay cancer-related assessments means that undiagnosed and untreated cancer cases continue to swell and compound with each wave of the pandemic. At best, the unfortunate result is a delay in treatment; at worst, it means untold suffering and deaths that could have been prevented.

This fact has been well-documented by several major research efforts. For example, according to the United Kingdom's Institute for Public Policy Research and Carnall Farrar (CF), it could take until the year 2033 to clear the cancer treatment backlog. Between March 2020 and February 2021, the number of referrals to see a specialist in the United Kingdom dropped by nearly 370,000 compared to the year before. This disaster must also take into account the thousands of people for whom a cure is no longer available because of the delay in diagnosis and treatment.[1]

In Canada, the predicted long-term impact of COVID-19 pandemic-related care delays on cancer mortality is wildly disturbing. Modelling suggests that for every 4-week delay in treatment, there is an additional 6 percent increase in the death rate. The prediction is that cancer care disruptions during the COVID-19 pandemic could amount to 21,247 more cancer deaths in Canada for the 10 year period between 2020 to 2030.[2]

As we collectively find our footing in a post-pandemic world, the impact on cancer care will last for many years. So, now more than ever, it is exceedingly important to seek medical assessment right away for any concerning symptoms because the sooner you enter the health care system for a cancer-related issue, the better your chances of the cancer being addressed at the earliest possible opportunity. A reduction in time to diagnosis and treatment = an increased chance to achieve remission or cure.

And with that, let's now turn our attention to treatments.

TREATMENT OPTIONS

Many different types of treatments can be used to help anyone survive cancer. Over the years, these methods have developed and been refined, while new ones are continuously being invented, tested, and refined further.

Chemotherapy[3]

First and foremost in popularity is chemotherapy. Chemotherapy has been used to treat cancers for many years. It is a type of cancer treatment that uses drugs to kill cancer cells, and it can treat cancer or reduce symptoms. It can be used as a stand-alone treatment or part of a combination. Some cancers are more responsive to chemotherapy than others.

Unfortunately, chemotherapy is associated with many side effects because chemotherapy drugs kill cancer cells *and* healthy cells, too. The good news is that most side effects are reversible and will stop when the chemotherapy treatment ends.

Radiotherapy[4]

Radiotherapy or radiation therapy involves using high doses of radiation to kill cancer cells. Radiotherapy has side effects, and there is also a lifetime dose limit that needs to be considered.

Surgery[5]

Surgery is used as a treatment when cancer forms a tumour and is localized. Apart from traditional surgeries involving scalpels and knives, there are newer forms of surgery, such as cryosurgery, lasers, hypothermia, and photodynamic therapy, and it can be open or minimally invasive. Surgery can remove the entire tumour, debulk a tumour, or relieve symptoms of the disease.

It is important to note that surgery cannot generally be used for blood cancers or cancers that have already spread to many parts of the body.

Over time, newer approaches have been adopted. Most of them involve precision medicine and personalized treatments; others aim to help the patient's immune system identify and destroy cancer cells.

Immunotherapy[6]

Immunotherapy is a kind of cancer treatment that supports your immune system in fighting cancer. There are many types of immunotherapies, including immune checkpoint inhibitors, T-cell transfer therapy, monoclonal antibodies, treatment vaccines, and immune system modulators. Immunotherapy is an emerging form of cancer treatment, and research is ongoing.

Some areas being researched include how to prevent or overcome treatment resistance, how to predict the response to immunotherapy; how cancer cells avoid immune responses and what can be done about it, and how to reduce the side effects of immunotherapy.

Stem Cell Transplants

Stem cell transplants are used to restore blood-forming stem cells to the body after they have been depleted during chemotherapy or radiotherapy. They are often adjuncts combined with other treatments, but in some leukemias and myeloma, stem cell transplants fight the cancer directly.[7]

There are three types of stem cell transplants. The first is autologous; this is a transplant when the stem cells come from you, the patient. The second is syngeneic, in which the transplant includes stem cells that come from an identical twin. And the third is allogeneic; this is a transplant when the stem cells come from a donor who may or may not be related to you.

No matter the type, stem cell transplants are often used to treat people with lymphoma, leukemia, multiple myeloma, or neuroblastoma.

Just like any kind of treatment, they can cause side effects, such as an increased risk of infections or bleeding. There is also the possibility that the host body cells will reject the transplant, a condition called graft-versus-host disease. Graft-versus-host is less likely to occur when the donor's stem cells match yours closely. If it happens, your doctors will manage this with medication, such as steroids.

It should be noted that stem cell transplant treatments for other cancers are undergoing research in clinical trials.

Targeted Therapy

Targeted therapy is a new kind of cancer treatment that targets the proteins responsible for cancer cell growth. Most targeted treatments are either small molecule drugs or monoclonal antibodies. Small molecule drugs are minuscule enough to easily enter cells, allowing them to attack targets *inside* cancer cells. Monoclonal antibodies, on the other hand, are proteins produced in the lab, designed to attach to specific targets found *on* cancer cells.

Some monoclonal antibodies mark cancer cells so that they will be better seen and destroyed by the immune system. Think of this as a way to highlight the cancer cells with bright yellow highlighter so that the immune system can easily find them. Other monoclonal antibodies are designed to directly stop cancer cells from growing or cause them to self-destruct, while the third class is designed to carry toxins in their payload to obliterate the target cancer cells.[8]

For a patient to benefit from either type of targeted therapy, the cancer must be tested to see if it contains targets for the drugs. Testing a cancer for targets is called biomarker testing—more on that below.

Targeted therapy fights cancer in several ways by effectively helping the immune system to stop cancer cells from thriving; it inhibits the signals that form blood vessels to nourish the cancer cells; it delivers cancer-killing compounds directly to the cancer cells; it causes cancer cells to die; and it starves cancer cells of the hormones they need to grow.[3]

Targeted therapy does have its drawbacks. Cancer cells can adapt to the treatment and develop a kind of resistance, therefore making some treatments ineffective over time. Also, drugs for some targets are not yet available to the public or have yet to be developed. There are also many physical side effects to targeted therapy.

DIAGNOSTIC TOOLS

Apart from new and improved treatment methods, there has been considerable advancement in the area of diagnostic tools for cancer treatment. These tools assist a medical team in determining which types of treatments may work best on an individual level.

Biomarker Testing

Biomarker testing is referred to by some as tumour testing, tumour genetic testing, genomic testing, molecular testing/profiling, hot-spot testing, somatic testing, or tumour subtyping. Biomarker testing is a way to identify tumour markers that can provide critical pieces of information about a cancer.[9] It is a vital part of precision medicine (also known as personalized medicine) because it helps to inform doctors about which drugs or clinical trials (if any) are available for one's specific cancer.

While select biomarker testing is available for both solid and blood tumours, its usefulness is limited because it only looks at the alterations (if any) on one gene. It can be useful for some patients; however, because cancer most often hijacks multiple genes, very important information may be missed if other genes are not assessed. If doctors don't have a comprehensive understanding of what is driving the cancer's growth, treatment options may be missed, and survival may be impacted. In most places, biomarker testing is not a routine form of cancer care; therefore, it would be wise if you discussed it with your doctor to assess for clinical viability in your case.

As good as biomarker testing is, it still remains a tool with limited (albeit important) information. It is by no means a panacea for cancer care. Sometimes, the testing does not find any biomarkers that have any available treatments. Sometimes, the treatment identified fails to work for unknown reasons. Sometimes, the biomarkers in a cancer change over time and no longer respond to previously matched treatments. Despite these risks, it is worth discussing the option of biomarker testing with your doctor or oncologist. Biomarker testing is available free as part of some clinical trials.

Comprehensive Genomic Profiling/Next-Generation Sequencing

The science that underpins this technology is one of the key reasons I am alive today. While this diagnostic and matching tool may not be applicable to every cancer patient, I firmly believe that it will continue to prove its value for many others.

I have said many times in various speeches, discussions, and meetings that if you have to deal with a cancer diagnosis, now is the best time in human history to do so. And the reason for that is found within the life-saving advantages of comprehensive genomic profiling. Understanding the key principles of this cutting-edge diagnostic tool may be an invaluable and life-saving resource, informing your important decisions regarding what treatment options or clinical trials may be best for you.

If biomarker testing is new, then next-generation sequencing (NGS) is ultramodern. NGS is an emerging biomedical technology that allows doctors to test many cancer genes at the same time. NGS can be conducted on cancer tissue that has been biopsied or surgically removed. In some solid tumours, it is also possible to test for small amounts of tumour DNA in the blood, referred to as a liquid biopsy.[10]

The advantages of NGS over individual biomarker tests are many.[11] As stated, NGS provides an opportunity to test many genes at once, saving time, money, and effort. But perhaps even more important is that it may accelerate new insights into your cancer type and subtype(s). Furthermore, in addition to the specific suspected biomarkers, it can identify *new* biomarkers, potentially increasing the scope of available treatment options. Since NGS is a relatively new diagnostic and matching modality, it does have some disadvantages. For instance, some NGS testing takes longer than individual biomarker testing. Individual biomarker testing takes a week or less; NGS can take up to three weeks. What's more, there is a cost, which is usually several thousands of dollars. Some insurers cover all or a portion of the test, so check with your insurance benefits administrator if this is something that they cover. In addition, it can be challenging to interpret the results of NGS, which can affect treatment choices. Your oncologist is one of the health professionals trained to correctly interpret your NGS results.

I feel compelled to share an important resource should you and/or your doctor feel that genomic assessment of your cancer may be of value. While several companies specialize in NGS either directly or indirectly, it's not in the scope of this book to promote one company over another. That said, if you are interested in pursuing NGS, a great place to start is Access to Comprehensive Genomic Profiling (ACGP). They have organized themselves to be a collaborative coalition of leading molecular diagnostics companies with the aim of achieving the following mission:

Access to Comprehensive Genomic Profiling (ACGP) aims to raise awareness about comprehensive genomic profiling (CGP) for advanced cancer patients. The coalition seeks to educate stakeholders about the value of CGP tests in all tumour types, to assure appropriate use in the patient journey, to inform medical management and improve clinical outcomes.[12]

ACGP is dedicated to sharing the clinical utility and economic value of CGP with healthcare stakeholders with the view of increasing access to this innovative technology, particularly in the United States. A lot of the information found on their website will apply to most cancer patients who are considering NGS assessment, regardless of where they live. They have some great FAQs, and they identify the companies within their membership that can help you discover the best treatment for your cancer.

For more information, visit ACGP at https://accesstocgp.com. I've also included this link as well as a QR code you can scan with your mobile device in Appendix C, so you can refer back to this and other online resources at any time. I hope you will find them useful.

EXPERIMENTAL TREATMENTS

As I mentioned earlier, scientists are constantly looking for better ways to fight cancer and searching for that elusive prize—a cure. Even now, many experimental treatments are being tested.

CAR-T Therapy

Chimeric antigen receptor T-cell therapy (CAR-T) is a remarkably promising cancer treatment developed in recent years. CAR-T is a form of immunotherapy that uses immune T cells from the patient's body to fight cancer by genetically engineering them to recognize cancer cells or specific proteins.[13]

It involves extracting, modifying, and replicating T-cells, then reintroducing them into the body to fight the cancer cells. CAR-T has been approved for use in treating some lymphomas and leukemias, and a limited number of cancer centres are authorized to provide the service. Scientists are testing this therapy on many other types of cancer.

In fact, a small but important study released results in February 2022 suggesting that CAR-T cell therapy may be a "curative regimen" for chronic lymphocytic leukemia (CLL), which comprises about 25 percent of leukemia cases. Although there were only two study participants, the CAR-T cells remained detectable more than ten years after they were infused back into the two patients. I am extremely encouraged by this new information because people with CLL may have a new and proven treatment option to help extend their lives.

New Drug Therapies

Several new drugs are being studied for their ability to treat cancers.[14] While the medications listed below are by no means endorsed by me, they serve as examples of the sorts of pharmacological drugs that have shown results sufficient enough to warrant further investigation.

- *Dichloroacetate:* Dichloroacetate has been shown to reduce tumours in mice. It kills cancer cells by inducing apoptosis, also known as programmed cell death. Preclinical trials for dichloroacetate are promising, but a full clinical trial has yet to be published. Thus, clinicians have yet to receive approvals for routine use of dichloroacetate. Improper use can lead to grievous side effects like liver damage; it should only be used in a controlled environment under specialist supervision.[15]
- *Quercetin:* Quercetin is a naturally occurring compound present in many fruits and vegetables. It acts as an antioxidant, scavenging free radicals, and is used as a dietary supplement. It has shown some anti-cancer effects on oral cancer and leukemia in the lab. Efforts are being made to create a Quercetin-based medication to fight cancer.[16]
- *Opdivo and Yervoy:* Opdivo and Yervoy are new anti-cancer medications that boost the immune system's ability to fight

cancers. They were approved for use in 2015.[17] Opdivo (nivolumab) is a programmed cell death receptor and a monoclonal antibody. It blocks antibodies and has been used to treat unresectable melanoma and some types of lung cancer. Yervoy is a monoclonal antibody that activates the immune system to fight cancer. It has been approved as a treatment for melanoma, and clinical trials are underway to see how effective and safe it is for use against other cancer types. When doctors offered both drugs to the first person to try them, they saw his melanoma tumours disappear within three weeks of receiving the first dose. In a larger trial involving 142 people, 22 percent of participants saw their cancers disappear completely.[18] Unfortunately, despite this high success rate, this drug combination is highly toxic.[19] However, these drugs are available for patients with advanced disease where the benefits of using the drugs are likely to outweigh the risks.

Bacterial Therapies and Virotherapy

As we saw in Chapter 4, bacteria and viruses have been used to induce remission of cancers in humans since the 1900s. Doctors abandoned earlier cancer treatments based on these agents because they were hard to control, and it was often impossible to predict the outcome. Besides, there were newer, more predictable treatments.[20]

Modern scientists have modified earlier treatments and developed bacterial and viral strains specifically to fight cancers.[21] Even with modifications, there have been cases of patients getting sepsis and gangrene from bacterial agents and passing away from those complications. However, safety measures have now been established to help reduce this from happening.

These are not the only methods of treatment for cancers, nor is this all of the information about these treatments. When it comes to any kind of treatment, you are advised to discuss your options at length with your medical team. You should also do your own research and keep an open mind to various treatment options. What may work for some may not work for others (and vice versa).

What's more, you should keep your eyes open for clinical trials and treatments. Clinical trials are real-time experiments with human beings using novel drugs that may be of tremendous value. They help doctors find better treatments for cancers and other diseases, and they can help you gain access to new or experimental therapies that might help you achieve remission. When there seems to be no hope left, many individuals will enter clinical trials not only to help themselves survive their own cancer but help add to the growing body of cancer research with the view of helping others.

There are several stages of clinical trials. Before clinical trials are conducted, preclinical or laboratory studies must be completed.

- *Phase 0:* This phase explores the possibility that a new drug might work.
- *Phase I:* This phase is to determine if the treatment is safe.
- *Phase II:* This phase is to check if the treatment works.
- *Phase III:* This phase compares the new treatment with existing treatments to determine if it is better.
- *Phase IV:* This phase explores long-term side effects, interactions with other conditions, and any other information needed before the drug can be approved for use on humans.

Treatments received as part of a clinical trial might help you live longer or even recover. More than 60 percent of children with cancer in the United States join a trial, and 75 percent of them live a long time after cancer. Many adults decide to join trials, and half of them enjoy an extension to their life after treatment, some for a long time.[22]

Presently, more than 380,000 registered clinical trials are being conducted in 220 countries. As of June 2021, about 40 percent of those trials were registered in the United States, while 60 percent were registered in 219 countries.[23]

These figures contrast sharply with the figures from earlier years. For example, in 2010, only 82,661 studies were registered, and in 2005, there were just 8,858.[24] This clearly indicates that the field of oncology research is rapidly advancing. We have better chances of surviving cancer now than we ever have before. I am a prime example and proud beneficiary of the rapid advancement in oncology research.

The first step to joining a clinical trial is to research it and discuss it with your doctor. With a little practice, you can search for clinical trials on your own. The websites are country-specific; however, many clinical trials have cross-over into other jurisdictions, thereby sometimes allowing patients to enrol from other countries. Some American clinical trials have satellite health centres that include clinical settings in Canada and other countries. Just be sure to look at credible websites; do not simply pick the first one you find without exploring other options.

One of the most popular clinical trial websites you may want to look into is from the American National Institute of Health's National Library of Medicine. It's an incredibly extensive database of privately and publicly funded clinical studies conducted around the world. It is very possible that the keys to a longer life could be found within this database. For more information, visit ClinicalTrials.gov at https://www.clinicaltrials.gov, or turn to Appendix C and scan the QR code on your mobile device.

All clinical trials have a protocol in which they spell out the criteria for joining. You will need to check if you meet the eligibility criteria before contacting the investigators. The National Cancer Institute has a checklist that helps you gather your information for easy access during screening; you can find a link and QR code to this resource in Appendix C, as well.

Deciding to participate in a clinical trial is not a process you should rush. Discussing it with friends and family members can help you weigh your options and identify the right questions to ask. It is also essential to talk to other doctors (apart from those in the trial) to gather well-informed, unbiased information.

The same philosophy can be applied to choosing your treatment method altogether. The more you know, the better you can advocate for yourself. And when it comes to surviving cancer, you need every advantage you can get.

Chapter 14 Notes

_____

_____

_____

_____

_____

_____

_____

_____

_____

_____

_____

_____

_____

_____

_____

CHAPTER 15

HAUNTED BY MY FUTURE

When my long course of radiation treatment was over, I was left with nothing but the question of what comes next.

Life had forced me to view the world through a much different lens. It was as though I had just gotten a new prescription for my glasses, and I needed to get used to them—but the images I was trying to see remained cloudy and obscured, in part because they focused on a dim future that I faced alone.

I watched as most of my friends continued their lives devoid of the profound existential threat I faced. Even my family continued with their lives as planned for the most part—and why wouldn't they? While I was very happy to see the people I loved live their lives while mine seemed to pause, I noticed the undeniable concern and palpable sense of worry they had for me and for themselves.

The question that put so much pressure on me had morphed from *whether* I would live to *how* exactly I would live. I did not know how much time I had ahead of me, so I wanted to hastily advance my life. I wanted to make plans for the future, not just for the day ahead. I wanted to begin working so that I could be self-sufficient. I wanted to marry, to become a dad, to have a partner to enjoy life's wonders with—to help each other cope with the inevitable difficulties.

In my youth, I had taken the future for granted, and now I was rushing to grab hold of it. This meant my goal of a career in the life sciences would be thwarted because that dream relied on a protracted amount of time in school. I felt that, rather than spending that time preparing for a professional career by seeking a postgraduate degree, I would use my precious time to live life and enjoy life's benefits now. Either way, I needed to complete my undergraduate program because it was important to me—and it was a short-term goal.

For about a year following the conclusion of my radiation treatments, I was assessed with blood tests and CT scans every three months, then every six months for three years, and finally just yearly.

These graduations of extending time between follow-up scans were both a blessing and a curse. On the one hand, the cancer seemed not to have returned. On the other hand, I had become so emotionally reliant on the medical community looking after me that I began to feel anxious as the length between appointments grew. I had forgotten how to live without scheduling my life around medical appointments and treatment sessions. I realized the appointments and sessions I dreaded during my treatment had become my security blanket throughout my journey—a security blanket that was now being pulled away.

Cancer patients know that surviving the first five years after treatment is a big deal. It's often met with words like "remission," "cure," or some other personal designation. I feel that everyone approaches the five-year mark slightly differently because, in the absence of disease, they choose to believe what they want to believe—what they must believe to cope with the news.

Personally, I lived those first five years with an incredible amount of fear. It was the kind of fear that is hard to describe. I was shaken to the core, and even as I write this book, the trauma of that fear washes over me. In truth, I had to pause the writing of this book several times because of the inherent difficulty in reliving that past. These aren't the sort of memories that fade with time. These traumatic experiences are as real today as they were 30 years ago.

The good news is that I did reach the five-year cancer-free mark, and that day was met with elation. It felt *incredible*. It felt as though I had won a hard-fought war.

But that sense of triumph was immediately replaced with feelings stemming from the non-stop emotional trauma. I felt that declaring victory would be tantamount to goading the cancer to return. I felt that, rather than poke the bear, I would offer this formidable foe the respect it had demanded of me. I didn't want any further trouble; I felt that a relationship based on mutual respect, despite the confrontation we'd had five years earlier, was the best path forward for the two of us.

The next 20 years included some life changes that anyone would have considered major, and in my case, their weight was compounded. Most notably, there was a move from Montreal, Quebec, to Toronto, Ontario, where I established a relationship with the Princess Margaret Cancer Centre based on annual follow-up appointments.

Those annual appointments developed into a routine. First, there was always a blood test, then a little wait in the lymphoma clinic, followed by a brief face-to-face with the radiation oncologist, who assumed my ongoing care. He was an affable gentleman, professional yet approachable—young enough to relate to me but old enough to command immediate respect.

Each year I met with him, it seemed that he regarded me as an example of radiation success. In a clinic where bald people outnumbered those with hair, I represented a breath of fresh air on my doctor's list of patients to see that day. I was faced with the pressure of continuing to be this shining example, yet with each year I spent cancer-free, I felt more comfortable in this role. I ventured a little farther from cancer, begrudgingly lengthening the leash by which I was tethered to the disease.

Yet still, the tether was there. The battle continued inside me.

I was reminded of my battle when I looked at my own image but also when I looked at the people around me. The ongoing nature of the threat to my life and family was at times excruciating. My empathetic nature was wounded each time I realized how much the possibility of my cancer's return would affect those I loved. The support from my friends and family simultaneously helped keep me going but also made my guilt grow. I felt responsible for their anticipated sadness and the stress I had assigned to them.

I knew living was a good thing. I knew that my thriving, my continued survival on the battleground of my body was a good thing. But it came with such a high cost that I couldn't stop invasive thoughts, wondering if it was worth it—if I was strong enough to handle the ongoing threat to my mind, my body, and my loved ones. So I did something about it.

In 1998, I sought out a cancer support group for young adults because that demographic has unique challenges: dating, finishing school, beginning a career, and many others. In Canada, a cancer support centre called Wellspring is available at no charge to help cancer patients, caregivers, and family members elevate their quality of life through a strengthened mind and body.

I was lucky to have participated in a 12-week-long young adult group of eight people led by Dr. Mavis Himes, a highly regarded clinical psychologist and psychoanalyst and author of two books. I engaged deeply in our weekly sessions and put much of what we learned into daily practice. And by the end of the sessions, Dr. Himes asked if I would like to work with her as a co-facilitator for future young adult groups.

I accepted the role and was quickly trained to become the best co-facilitator I could be. Together, Dr. Himes and I worked closely with many other young adult cancer patients. They benefited from my presence in part because it was encouraging for them to see that one could survive cancer. I was a living, breathing example of survival, a bright light of much-needed hope for them. Every single young adult I met during those groups left an incredible impression on me. However, during our annual get-togethers, some were notably absent because, tragically, they died very early in life.

Almost 25 years later, I remain in contact with Dr. Himes. There was one young adult I befriended—Eric, a budding photographer, just starting his career. I promised him that should I be lucky enough to have children, I would hire him to be the photographer at family functions. In 2017 and 2019, Eric was the photographer at my children's Bar and Bat Mitzvahs, and I recently met his new baby girl.

I can't recommend enough that those who are fighting or have fought cancer get involved with a support group. Visit the Wellspring website at https://wellspring.ca to find locations and programs near you. You can also find this link and a QR code in Appendix C.

Still, while my work at Wellspring was meaningful, I was haunted by my future. I was holding onto a fear of what was coming. It wasn't the fear of not being able to win the war; rather, it was the fear that I *would* win. Every corner I turned, I was faced with the question of whether my body and mind could recover. I feared that my body would return home from the war, but my mind would stay on the battlefield, unable to fully enjoy life.

But this fear of the future was not my biggest fear or emotional anguish during that period of my life. My greatest fear of all wasn't that I'd lose the fight by losing my life. In fact, my greatest fear wasn't for me at all.

My greatest anguish was and is that I would die before one or both of my parents. My parents had already outlived one of their children. How could I put them through that again? Not only did I feel responsible for my own future, but I felt responsible for my parents' futures, too.

Chapter 15 Notes

CHAPTER 16

AND THE BEAT GOES ON

When it comes to our bodies, there are many things that we tend to take for granted. We cannot be entirely blamed for this. Many of our bodily functions happen automatically and therefore don't garner our attention. Out of sight, out of mind, right? We begin to notice them, their importance, and their power only when we are inconvenienced or when these automatic functions are threatened.

Perhaps the most obvious example of this is when you have a cold. Among other symptoms, the common cold usually includes a congested nose and a sore throat. As a result, one nostril is likely to be blocked, and the act of swallowing can become compromised and painful. In these moments, many individuals become grateful for those times before the cold, when they swallowed without pain and were able to breathe through their nose without trouble. Following their return to health, they again ignore the automatic functions of their body. They forget just how much their body does for them on a regular basis, only to remember once more when the cold inevitably returns.

I, too, was a victim of this blindness when it came to my own struggle with cancer.

Following the remission of my Hodgkin's disease, several things changed in my life. As I've said, I was eager to live my life, and I did so. After I completed my undergraduate degree, I felt that the path of least resistance was to enter the workforce and join my family's established business, which I always found intriguing. I moved to Toronto in 1994 and quickly assumed more responsibilities within the business, eventually leading ongoing sales, management, and the overall direction of our company. We were in the business of helping other companies market their products and services through the process known as sales promotion marketing. This discipline occupies a very narrow but highly specialized area within the realm of promotion marketing, and I thoroughly enjoyed working with clients using innovative and engaging techniques to achieve (and in many cases exceed) their business goals. One of the things I am most proud of was transitioning the company from using traditional marketing tactics to the effective use of digital means. This transition modernized the company and provided the necessary pivot for traditional companies to maintain their relevance in the age of digital marketing.

I married my former wife in 1997, and we had two beautiful children together: Ethan in 2004 and Hila in 2007. In keeping with my life's theme of hardship and challenge, the marriage needed to end, and from 2008 to 2012, I was embroiled in a protracted and messy divorce, the likes of which I never imagined I would have to face. That said, my new title and responsibility of being a single dad was the best thing that happened to me and helped propel me forward.

As most parents know, having children changes life in the best way possible. I couldn't believe that I had made it to fatherhood. I promised myself that I would be the best dad I could be because my children deserve it. Becoming a parent is an incredible feeling, but *me* becoming a parent seemed to carry with it an extra amount of profound responsibility. Just as I felt guilty about the possible impact on my greater family should I die early in life, this guilt now extended to my children.

Was I selfish to want to bring new life into the world, knowing that I could die early in life? I thought carefully about that for a long time. Ultimately, my rationalization turned to the harsh reality of life: anyone could die at any time, and in that context, I was no different than any other parent. But it seemed my constant attention to my own mortality was not something most people my age shared. Warranted or not, healthy or not, my ongoing elation in becoming a parent was always met with a self-imposed lingering feeling of selfishness and concern for those I would leave behind. Would my kids be okay should I pass away early in life? That question would drive me to embrace the precious moments of fatherhood, incredibly satisfying moments that persist and will continue until my last breath.

In April of 2013, a mutual friend introduced me to Cynthia. I was 43 years old, soon to be 44, and during the evening of April 10, I reached out to Cynthia via a text message. We arranged to meet at a restaurant two days later, on April 12, for our first date. That date went so well that we left the restaurant and went to two other places together that evening. We couldn't wait to see each other again, so the following day, on our second date, Cynthia suggested that we go to a venue where about 25 of her friends were attending a live performance. Without so much as a flinch, I accepted, figuring I would meet her friends at some point, anyway—so if Cynthia was offering now, I was game. Her friends were great, and we all thoroughly enjoyed ourselves. My intuition was screaming that I had met a very special person in Cynthia.

After my divorce, I changed my diet and my lifestyle completely. I was determined to become the picture of good health; no other health crisis would happen to me for a very long time, I thought. I would show my body how to be healthy. I would show it how much I appreciated what it had done for me, helping to fight off the cancer. I had to. I was in my early 40s—the prime of my life—with my two beautiful young children and an incredibly special person by my side in Cynthia. It was finally my time to live the life I wanted so desperately to have.

In the two decades that followed my first war with cancer, I pushed my body to be in the best physical shape of my life. I took up running and did so at least four times a week. I even entered and competed in a half-marathon (21.1 km) in 2012.

The success and joy I found in running allowed me to begin to trust my body once more. I felt like I had before my diagnosis of Hodgkin's disease. I was finally able to place trust in the body that was hijacked by cancer. Physically, you wouldn't have known I had fought the hardest battle of my life twenty years earlier.

In this way, I began to forget what my body had gone through. The traumatic memories of my cancer treatments began to be mere remembrances, no longer plaguing my mind. They no longer flashed in my view when I closed my eyes or wasn't paying attention. With the exception of one day per year when I would attend the Princess Margaret Cancer Centre for my annual follow-up, I no longer felt like a cancer patient. I was a regular, healthy person—or so I thought.

Just when I began to forget the battle of the past, I was reminded once more that life has a way of interfering with the best of plans.

In keeping with the trajectory of my life, on May 8, 2013, I drove myself to a local hospital because I was having chest pain. This pain was unlike anything I had experienced before, and I knew it was not normal. I texted Cynthia from the waiting room of the ER and downplayed the issue. However, it didn't take long before my ER visit quickly turned into an emergency hospital admission because I was having a heart attack.

Yes, you read that correctly: three weeks after meeting Cynthia, I had a heart attack at the age of 43 as a single dad with children ages nine and six. There's a lot to unpack there, but I don't want to detract from the focus of the book. The reason I include this is to offer some interesting and noteworthy details of a life not devoid of interesting detail and experiences. I could write an entire book about the heart attack itself, but the important point is that I survived that, too, and it made my bond with Cynthia that much more special.

I didn't want to tell my family and worry my parents, who were six hours away in Montreal, but they had to know in case I died. As awful as that thought is, imagine feeling what I was feeling: scared, alone, worried about my kids' future without a dad, and wanting to protect my parents from unimaginable worry.

My emergency heart attack required the installation of two cardiac stents to open the blockages. As I lay on the surgical table, fully awake and aware in the cardiac catheterization suite at Sunnybrook Health Sciences Centre—and all throughout my recovery—I was forced to relive memories of my previous cancer treatments, reminded that there are processes in our body we do not see and, therefore, take for granted.

Throughout my first cancer battle, my heart was never an explicit problem, so it was never a worry for me. I was more worried about the cancer spreading to other parts of my body than whether my heart could manage the insult of the radiation.

Even in the decades that followed my first cancer, when I attempted to honour my body by becoming healthy, my heart was the last thing on my mind. It wasn't until my heart failed during a run that I became aware of how much my heart had done for me when I wasn't paying attention. It had gotten me through a battle that many people do not win. It had gotten me to a place of health and peace.

After many tests, it was finally revealed why my heart had failed me. I had developed underlying heart disease as a direct consequence of the radiation treatment I received in 1991. As it turns out, the radiation that had been so focused on my upper mantle area weakened my heart. Then, as I began running, while the rest of my body was becoming healthy, the strain on my heart was too much. Ever so slowly, the tissues of my cardiovascular system were reacting to the repeated radiation to my chest in 1991.

I was reminded that while we may forget what we have gone through, the body doesn't forget what has happened to it. From that point on, there were a few lessons that have stayed with me.

The first is that I have vowed to never again take for granted what my body does for me on a day-to-day basis. This vow has been easy to uphold as I now frequently hear and pay attention to the beat of my heart within my chest. As of the publishing of this book, my heart is once again showing signs of stress with an irregular heartbeat, and I am in the all-too-familiar arena of cardiac follow-up. It is my full intention to get this sorted out.

The second is that, after facing so much adversity, so many challenges and threats, I have gained a new appreciation for the phrase "the beat goes on."

Chapter 16 Notes

_____

_____

_____

_____

_____

_____

_____

_____

_____

_____

_____

_____

_____

_____

_____

CHAPTER 17

THE SECOND COMING

After the heart attack, I confidently assumed I was free from any more health crises, at least for a while; surely, two major health crises in such a short period of time were enough for one person. I was grossly mistaken. Little did I know that these were just a warm-up, preparing me for the hardest battle yet.

Three years after my 2013 heart attack, I discovered a lump on the right side of my neck. This set the stage for the latter half of 2016, the next act in the Shit Show. Through a fine needle biopsy of that lump, it was confirmed cancerous—though what type of cancer it was had yet to be determined.

I could not believe this was happening again. Life had changed since my battle with Hodgkin's disease, and this change was mostly good— very good. I was still alive. Alive *and* kicking. Surviving cancer for 25 years isn't just about surviving, particularly as a young adult. It's about developing the emotional wherewithal to weather the inevitable difficult moments certain to come along in life. However, if there's one event that takes the wind out of one's sails, it's the diagnosis of another cancer. While I am grateful for those 25 years of life, nothing could prepare me for what was to come.

I was sent to a head and neck oncology surgeon at the Princess Margaret Cancer Centre - the same hospital where I'd had annual follow-up visits for my Hodgkin's disease after my radiation treatment so many years ago. There, the surgeon performed what is known as a neck dissection to assess the type of cancer and the extent of its spread. I was nervous about the process, yet there was an eerie sense of familiarity, like a recurring nightmare: I knew what was coming but was helpless to stop it. The extent of the neck dissection was as invasive as the cancer itself. Most of the more than 20 lymph nodes removed tested positive for cancer—and this was a bad cancer. A very, very bad cancer. This time, the cancer had dressed itself up as salivary duct carcinoma, and it made its presence known in an extremely aggressive way, spreading to neck muscles and surrounding tissue rather quickly.

This "second cancer" developed as yet another direct consequence of the radiation I had received 25 years earlier for the "first cancer"—yet another reason why my choice in treatment so many years ago haunted me for so long. The lymph nodes affected in my neck were now pregnant and swelling with one of the worst head and neck cancers one could suffer, and it was only about to get worse.

Despite the skilled hands of an amazing head/neck surgeon, the cancer ensured that I would always know of its presence: a hole was left following the removal of half of my right neck. As if that wasn't bad enough, I was also left with a slash across the underside of my throat. I looked like the victim of a knife fight. I had effectively been maimed for all to see and gawk at in public.

If you will indulge me with a slight digression, my resulting appearance used to bother me quite a bit. I felt as though I was an odd and unusual circus performer being paraded around for individuals to point and stare at. But now, I wear my maimed neck proudly as it represents part of my survivorship. How can't I be proud of that?

It is normal human behaviour to be drawn to the unusual. Like a moth that can't help itself, we are drawn to the flame. I understand how my neck attracts looks in public, and I accept it. I accept it just as I accept other types of behaviour as being part of the human condition. *Let people stare!* I say. This is my battle scar; this is proof that I faced death and won (so far); this is my souvenir for being alive.

My second cancer, salivary duct carcinoma, is a rare head and neck cancer with an absolutely abysmal survival rate, particularly when diagnosed at an advanced stage. In my case, after the surgical pathology was done, my cancer was labelled as stage-4, the most advanced stage possible. I had never felt so unlucky. With many lymph nodes involved, the cancer was thought to be metastatic, meaning there was a high likelihood that the cancer had already spread beyond the head and neck to other parts of my body.

Following the initial staging and diagnostic surgery, I underwent yet another aggressive course of radiation treatment to my head and neck. The usual head/neck radiation therapy has the patient visit the hospital once per day from Monday to Friday, and that's what I thought I was going to get. I was wrong. For me, my radiation oncologist wanted to give me the best chance of kicking this cancer out of my body. This meant I was to go to the hospital twice per day for two radiation treatments. From a practical point of view, travelling downtown twice per day would be less than ideal because, by the time I returned home to the suburbs from my morning treatment, I would need to get back into my car and head back downtown to attend my afternoon treatment. To address this logistical issue, I moved into a downtown hotel near the hospital.

I would not do the story justice if I didn't share a little-known fact when it comes to the evolution of head/neck radiation. As you know, my first bout of cancer in 1991 also included head/neck radiation, so I had some experience. I thought I knew what was coming in the way of treatment room preparation.

A few key concepts are needed for full effect. The field of radiation treatment is a highly specialized discipline that requires careful planning before any radiation is delivered. This is because the location and margins of tumours are different from patient to patient—plus, everyone's internal structures are shaped and located slightly differently. I mean to say that all organs and structures are in the same general area, but there are very small variations in size, shape, and location from person to person. Even though those differences are millimetres apart, the treatment can only be effective if the radiation is delivered precisely to the required areas—and speaking of delivery, the machine that drives the radiation into the tumour is generally referred to as a linear accelerator.

In 1991, the treatment plan was to map out my internal organs and create lead shielding where appropriate so that some parts of organs could be spared from the barrage of radiation. Once my internal organs were mapped, they permanently tattooed small areas of my front and back, then painted bright red ink all over my body. This was so that each day, the radiation technologist could consistently and reliably align my body underneath the linear accelerator, which was in a fixed position. The only things that could be adjusted back then were the position of my body on the table and the position of the table itself relative to the linear accelerator. The goal was to ensure that the tattoos and red outline paint were in the exact same position each day.

But there was one more thing. I affectionately referred to my 1991 radiation treatments as Shake n' Bake. For the first half of the treatment, I would lie on my back, instructed not to move—not even a centimetre —while the radiation was delivered to the front of my body. I called this the "shake" part. When that was done, the technician returned to the room and had me flip over. They then proceeded to line up the tattoos and red lines painted on my backside and instructed again not to move so that the radiation could be accurately delivered to the opposite side of my body—this, then, was the "bake" part.

So, fast forward 25 years, and some important things had changed with respect to the delivery of radiation. The main difference was that the linear accelerator was no longer in a fixed position. The head of the accelerator was now designed to rotate around the body. This was a huge leap forward because it allows the patient to remain in one position for the duration of the treatment while the machine does the work of moving and delivering the radiation to the appropriate areas.

Still, for head/neck patients, there's a bit of a quid pro quo involved. To enjoy the benefits of a one-and-done treatment position wherein the machine does all the moving, the head needs to be totally immobilized. So, at every treatment, a custom-made rigid mesh cage was put over my face and neck and literally screwed into the treatment table.

I invite you to close your eyes for a moment and picture a cage being put over your face and neck with the edges of the cage screwed into the table you are lying on. Then the technician leaves the room, and the linear accelerator starts slowly whizzing and whirling around your head.

Not only do you have cancer—not only are you scared for your very survival—but now, twice a day, you are literally *screwed into a table*, and the cage is so tight against your face, you can't so much as purse your lips.

This caused me a great deal of anxiety at every treatment. The difficulty of each treatment added to the next, and the anxiety built up to the point that I needed, on the advice of my radiation oncologist, to take anti-anxiety medicine before entering the treatment room.

Finally, the radiation treatments ended, and I felt the full effects. My mouth was peppered with painful sores, my throat was extremely raw (necessitating that I eat soft or blended foods), and my energy was sucked out of me. But, if you can believe it, I was lucky; the radiation was ipsilateral—meaning it was directed to only one side of my head/neck area. People who receive bilateral radiation (that is, to both sides of the head/neck) often require the installation of a temporary feeding tube because swallowing is simply impossible for a length of time until the effects of the radiation subside.

About 12 weeks passed after my final treatment before it was time to see if the radiation and surgery had been successful.

The good news was that, as a patient of the Princess Margaret Cancer Centre, both the radiation and the surgery were a resounding success. Both had been delivered to their exacting standards, no less than expected from one of the top five cancer research centres in the world.

The bad news was that the CT scans revealed the cancer had spread to my lungs and related lymph nodes. This was considered the worst possible scenario.

This was no fault of the highly professional cancer specialists. They did their jobs exceptionally well, but the cancer did its job better. Prior to my detection a few months earlier, the cancer had moved quickly and with purpose—first from my salivary gland, then to my lymph nodes, then to the surrounding muscle, and finally to my lungs. The proverbial expression about the horse leaving the barn can be applied here. Once cancer spreads to distant parts of the body, it's usually "game over."

In an attempt to offer me peace and closure, my medical care team at this point referred me to the care of the palliative services department— usually the final referral a cancer patient will receive—given the extent of the cancer spread and how the disease is expected to overrun the body. For me, this was the death knell, the final attempt of medical professionals to do what they could for me in an effort to make me as comfortable as possible. While they were determined to help me for as long as they could, it was clear they did not think my chances of survival were great. It was suggested that I begin planning for the end of my life because it looked like the cancer was poised to overrun my body in short order.

Prior to 2016, I had faced two major health crises, yet nothing could have prepared me for hearing the "T" word used so easily.

Mr. Chankowsky, I am sorry, but despite the aggressive surgery and radiation, your cancer has spread to your lungs, and it is now TERMINAL. Your cancer is extremely rare, and there is no standard of care anywhere in the world.

Chapter 17 Notes

_____

_____

_____

_____

_____

_____

_____

_____

_____

_____

_____

_____

_____

_____

_____

CHAPTER 18

HIGHER STAKES

That word: *TERMINAL.* It rings in your brain like the endless echo of a loud bell. You can cover your ears, muffle the sound, and distract your mind, but the ringing is always there. That word is always there.

Before this diagnosis, I had only used the word to describe that final station on a subway line. I was reminded of its more sombre usage with my second diagnosis. I have always known "terminal" could be used to describe that final stage of cancer just before death, but having it used to describe your *own* cancer evokes a new kind of relationship with the word.

You see, the word "terminal" didn't just apply to me and the severity of my cancer. The terminal nature of my cancer stretched beyond its effect on me and reached my family and my children. It foreshadowed the *termination* of my presence at birthday celebrations, school graduations, perhaps weddings—even the births of grandchildren. It heralded the end of my active role as father and signified the beginning of profound uncertainty for my young children.

Terminal shoved my parents into unimaginable emotional turmoil as they faced the real possibility of burying yet another child in the near future.

Terminal attacked the promise Cynthia and I made to one another for a long life together, filled with the love we had finally found in one another, threatening to make it unfulfilled.

Terminal was the harbinger of the end of lifelong and dear friendships with people I hold in high esteem and the premature end of a business I spent 25 years developing.

I was in no kind of emotional state to share this news with anyone close to me, yet I was navigating this diagnosis in real-time while the regular schedule of my parenting and daily life played out. The only person aware of the morose reality of this awful situation and my accompanying feelings was Cynthia.

I was never one to cry, but now, I cried in private—a lot—and sometimes with Cynthia. My emotions were occupying a place that I had never seen in myself, and although I knew I was in a new place, the fluorescence of paralyzing fear was unmistakably blinding. I couldn't see. I wanted to, but I just couldn't.

Yet every day, I awoke and donned my emotional armour. I was determined to protect my kids and family for as long as possible—until I was ready to reveal the facts and far-reaching implications of my disclosure—until I could help them manage the anticipatory anxiety of my untimely death.

While this approach parallels the emotional path I took during my first cancer diagnosis in 1991, when I needed to manage my own emotions before I was able to help others, the similarity stops there. This time, there were two huge differences: my kids, Ethan and Hila. They were twelve and nine years old, respectively, and not yet emotionally capable of receiving this news. So, my go-to approach was to wait to tell them for as long as I could.

Thankfully, the initial shock of this cancer diagnosis subsided much more quickly than it had the first time around. As much as I didn't want it to be so, this was familiar territory to me. It was a different cancer, and it was at a different time in my life, but this time, I had more to hold onto to steady me. This time, there weren't as many "unknowns."

When I pushed through the fog that was the shock of my second cancer diagnosis, I was surprisingly met with a world of motivation and hope. Even with modern medicine, when doctors designate the stage of cancer to be terminal, this usually signifies certain and imminent death to many. Indeed, *terminal* loomed over me like a rain cloud ready to pour—but my life had changed so much over the previous 25 years that the ground under my feet allowed me to steady myself. I was able to look forward positively; the rain be damned.

I had two children who were dependent on me and years of joy to look forward to with them, Cynthia, and our families. Imagine my elation at finally finding the love of my life, the one who had been holding the key to my heart all along, and then *this*—this terminal diagnosis?

I was not going to let that go so easily.

Don't get me wrong; the diagnosis was akin to the explosion of a nuclear bomb. The utter devastation made it difficult to breathe. These pillars in my life, my children and Cynthia, and our families didn't make my second diagnosis less important or less serious. They did give my life, however, more importance and even more relevance, adding to my reasons to push through.

The stakes were higher now, much higher than in 1991 with my first diagnosis. I couldn't die—not now. It didn't matter that the second hospital we attended in New York for a second opinion and the third hospital in Houston, for a third opinion confirmed this awful diagnosis; it wasn't my time to die. It *couldn't* be my time.

My greatest fears were that I wouldn't be able to fulfil my obligations as a father, as a son, as a life-partner, as a member of my family, and as a friend to so many. I feared that I wouldn't be able to fulfil the promise I made to myself 25 years earlier.

In 1991, I had vowed to live a complete life. I had vowed to live a life in which I was able to experience what most people experience. I was going to attend every school graduation and milestone for my children. I was going to walk my daughter down the aisle at her wedding, and I was going to give a rousing toast at my son's. I would be able to revel in the satisfaction of watching my children develop into well-rounded and functioning adults. I would witness with pride as they did what they loved in life, and I would help them through difficult life transitions with the emotional tools I'd tried so hard to instil in them.

Although those dreamy possibilities that every parent hopes for were disintegrating right in front of me, I was determined to hold on to them, not let them fade. I convinced myself these would still be possibilities for me while I faced my second diagnosis.

Even with this new depth of meaning to my life, even with these new reasons for living, I was faced with the realization that eliminating the cancer was no longer an option. *Terminal.* The cancer had freed itself from the confines of my head and neck and migrated to my lungs.

I had more reasons to fight this time, but the fight was going to be harder—something that I didn't fully appreciate until all hope was lost.

Chapter 18 Notes

CHAPTER 19

BEING THE ONE IN FIVE

One cancer diagnosis in a lifetime is more than enough. One health crisis in a lifetime is more than enough. In fact, one is *too* much. So, what is two? What is three? How does one cope with three major health crises? How does one cope with a health crisis when their medical team is signalling to prepare for the worst?

Since 1991, my life had taken some major turns and included some significant obstacles. By 2016, I was exhausted. Many people mentioned how fortunate I was to have already gone through cancer once.

"At least you know what's coming."

But I wasn't fortunate. How is knowing what comes next fortunate? Indeed, I knew the process. I knew the general tests and the road my treatment would take. But I also knew the pain, the frustration, and the immense emotional and physical trauma it would take to outlive my cancer diagnosis—if that was even possible.

My survival of Hodgkin's lymphoma and my heart attack was clouded by my new diagnosis of salivary duct cancer. This wasn't like the first time when I didn't know what had caused the mutation of cells. This time, I knew exactly what it was: it was my original cancer treatment. The stage was set. The radiation that had saved my life over two decades earlier would now likely take my life. The poetic irony was so incredibly frustrating. Imagine the feeling of finally meeting the ultimate consequence of my surviving Hodgkin's disease.

I could not let that happen to me. I couldn't let my greatest achievement and proudest moment—surviving cancer the first time—be my eventual downfall. I always appreciated poetic irony in movies, television, and nature, but it had no place in my life—until now.

This irony brought me back to a special location that I frequented often: The Koffler Scientific Reserve at Jokers Hill, in King City, Ontario —about an hour north of Toronto. With large swaths of tree-lined, untouched sprawling land, the fall season was particularly inviting. I was drawn to the location annually but more frequently as the change of season progressed deeper into autumn. I wanted to capture the feeling of what I was seeing. I saw bitter irony because the leaves, while incredibly captivating with their colours, were also dying. I called this location and the poem "My Little Oasis."

My Little Oasis

Meandering roads
up
and
down
braced by lines yellow and white
create a passage-way to a latent destination
that finally reveals itself.

Beyond a crest of lineless road, a multi-hued tree canopy
     emerges.
A sheltering usher to My Little Oasis.
The canopy bulk, recently rich with life, slowly recedes
     with breathtaking fatigue.

In private, two jokers jest on Joker's Hill.

An old tree and her sister sit alone, weeping by roads
    edge.
They watch horses graze on hills
rolling with freshly manicured grass.
Their colourful tears, haphazardly shedding, succumb to
    gravity –
each singular one heaving
one last plummeting gasp before
uniting in the patchwork blanket
beneath.

The assault slowly approaches.

In the distance, a bold and striking set of crimson cousins
    take turns screaming out for attention.
Their beacons repeatedly chant to all that it is safe to
    let go–
change is welcome and necessary.
Tears will create a clean canvas for next year's colour
    palate.

Tethered to My Little Oasis where the jesting jokers rest,
meandering roads
up
and
down
with lines yellow and white
follow me in my rearview mirror.

As the years went by, I would return to "My Little Oasis" regularly, most notably during the fall. As with any piece of writing—particularly poems—the feeling of the words change with the seasons of one's life. Even though I composed the poem, it evoked different emotions each year, which amazed me. As with life itself and the certainty of birth and death, the words of my poem never changed, but their feelings evolved over time—just as a person evolves during their lifetime. Today, in the winter of my life, the words held within "My Little Oasis" once again take on new meaning.

At the time of my terminal diagnosis, though, I was frustrated, and my frustration quickly turned into panic and fear. Would I be able to survive cancer again? The word *terminal* really made it seem like I wasn't going to.

I would have this for the rest of my life, no matter how long or short that would be. I would never be able to rid my body of this disease; it had too strong a hold. It was in my lungs and my neck and G-d only knew where else. It would not be much longer before it was in other parts of my body, further strengthening its grip, successful in its goal of upending the lives of those who mean so much to me.

I was faced with an all-too-familiar dilemma. If I didn't find a solution to extend my life beyond the hopelessness found in the dismal statistics, it was game over. I couldn't bring myself to the point where I was able to have frank discussions with my family and friends about the dire seriousness and urgency of my medical problems. How could I put them through this—again—especially when there was little possibility of hope? I had to protect my parents at all costs for as long as possible.

There was one person I had no choice but to tell from the beginning. Cynthia was my greatest and most fearless cheerleader. She was the one next to me, holding my hand, as I stood to face death yet again. She noticed right away that my motivation was dwindling, at risk of becoming extinct completely. She was the one who chose—for both of us —that cancer, although it had a strong hold on my body for the time being, would not and would never again have a strong hold on my mind.

Even while she carried my secret with her for so long, her conviction never wavered, and her positivity never faded. She was the bright sun shining through the dark cloud that seemed to follow me around.

Statistically speaking, when it came to my stage and grade of cancer, my chances of surviving for five years was 20 percent at best. This news hit me like a bomb; it took everything I had not to focus on how low that percentage was. But Cynthia wouldn't entertain my negativity—wouldn't even hear it. Instead of thinking about the four out of five people who would perish and succumb to this fight, she was focused on the one in five who would live past five years.

When I would ask, "Why would *I* be the one person out of five to live past five years?" she would say, "Why *can't* you be that one person out of five who lives?'

I could tell in her tone that she wasn't *just* sure I would be the one person in five to live past five years; she was sure I would live much, much longer. Although I had no idea where she got her certainty, courage, and positivity, I had to admit that her point was a good one. Who says I couldn't be the one out of five? The challenge now was figuring out how to become that one person.

We quickly got to work figuring out how to survive cancer once more.

Chapter 19 Notes

_____

_____

_____

_____

_____

_____

_____

_____

_____

_____

_____

_____

_____

_____

CHAPTER 20

TAKING MY LIFE INTO MY OWN HANDS

Together, Cynthia and I decided that we needed to take my life, my body, and my mind back from cancer's grip. After some rather intensive research on our parts, we developed a plan. It began with finding out as much as we could about my rare cancer. We figured that the more we knew about it, the better chance we had to be the victors in our battle.

We worked closely with the Princess Margaret Cancer Centre in Toronto to have my tumour sent to a highly specialized lab, where it would be assessed for any actionable genetic mutations. This is often referred to as next-generation sequencing (NGS) or genomic biomarker testing, as discussed in Chapter 14. The final lab report, which held part of the keys to what may be driving my cancer's growth, was delivered on October 17, 2016, only a few months after the initial discovery of the tumour. We reviewed the results together with the newest member of our team, Dr. Lillian Siu. Among other significant awards and research interests, Dr. Siu is a world-renowned cancer expert with a particular interest in phase I trials on anti-cancer drugs and head & neck malignancies.

According to the lab report, my tumour revealed four genetic mutations. Unfortunately, at that time, only two of the tumour's four genetic mutations were "druggable," to use Dr. Siu's words—meaning that only two were targetable using the best available drugs. What's more, the drugs used to target the mutations were harsh and not particularly appealing, even in the context of a life-extending cancer treatment.

The news worsened: since the overall quantity of mutations within my tumour was low, this meant that immunotherapy as a possible treatment was expected to have little to no effectiveness. One by one, the few known treatment options for my rare cancer were being eliminated. Once again, panic was setting in, and dread began to come over us.

I had a choice to make: either I would have to accept becoming another victim of a rare cancer for which no treatment was available, or I would have to think outside the box and try to identify other viable options to extend my life.

Even if I failed, I needed to satisfy myself that no stone was left unturned. I could not die thinking that there was something that could have helped. With our new conviction, Cynthia and I set out together to do as much research as we could and find out as much as possible about this notoriously aggressive cancer.

Although neither of us is a medical professional, we needed to approach the research as if we were. Reading hundreds of medical journals, reports, and articles from anywhere we could find them was the objective. We used our mobile phones and computers to scour the planet for all information about salivary duct cancer. We nearly blinded ourselves with the out-of-reach medical jargon and thousands of statistics, but we were determined to find something—anything—we could use.

Most of the reports we came across echoed the consensus about this disease that there was little if any hope for prolonging my life. However, we remembered from the neck dissection surgical report that there was one feature of the tumour that stood out, and we came across that feature in just two or three small reports. The feature in question was that my cancer was fuelled by androgen hormones. The medical term pathologists use to refer to this is *androgen receptor-positive*. In everyday language, as we found out, when a cancer is androgen receptor-positive, the approach is simple: starve the tumour of androgen hormones, and the cancer will then slow its spread and growth.

When we saw these small studies on salivary duct carcinoma involving androgen receptor-positive drivers fueling the growth of the tumour, we knew that we had likely stumbled on a breakthrough. We were all but certain that we had found our last string of hope, and we were determined to make something out of it.

With this, we focused our energies on seeking out any information on cancers fuelled by androgens. We conducted our search with a voraciousness, the likes of which I had never experienced. We quickly learned how to read medical journals and scan them for the nuggets of pertinent information we were looking for. We focused only on legitimate medical journals, those that were peer-reviewed or had some other professional designation of medical authority and legitimacy. These journals and reports were highly specific and chock-full of medical terminology. Though they were difficult to get through, we had no time for uncredited or biased research. Our time was precious. I didn't want to spend my last few years doing research that resulted in nothing.

We learned quickly that the anatomy of a medical research report was broken down into two main components: the abstract and the body of the report. Being able to quickly assess the value of a research report through a quick glance at its abstract soon became second nature to us. Any value contained within a research journal would be identified within its abstract. Therefore, if there was even a *hint* of a lead within the abstract, we would dig deeper and weed through the minutiae of its details in the body to hopefully shed light on the information we sought.

We looked at many research reports dealing with salivary duct carcinoma—but there weren't very many because this cancer is so incredibly rare that assembling enough people to compose a legitimate research report is difficult, if not impossible. The available research patient populations for salivary duct carcinoma generally range from as few as eight to as many as fifty. These numbers are laughable within the research community. What conclusions could one reasonably expect to make with such low numbers of patients? What was I to do?

Cynthia and I came across a few legitimate reports dealing with androgen receptor-positive salivary duct carcinoma, for which there were drugs showing great success, but the low number of patients made the research seem statistically irrelevant. No matter—we continued on with our search. The thing with rare cancers is that the best we could hope for was some overlap of common tumour features with other "mainstream" cancers. So, we looked at many other cancers that have androgens as their primary driver. These reports were significantly more plentiful because more people were getting these mainstream cancers.

Between these two categories of research, we must have sifted through well over 100 studies that had androgen receptor features associated with the cancer. Eventually, we were able to target our research on combining the best of these two categories to see if there was any overlap.

We began to come across research reports dealing with androgen receptor-positive prostate cancer. These reports had patient populations more in line with what's regarded as statistically meaningful. In addition, we came across research reports dealing with androgen receptor-positive invasive ductal breast cancer that also had large numbers of patient populations. It was slowly becoming clearer to us that any therapy worth trying would be hormone-based chemotherapy.

Cancers used to be treated as a one-size-fits-all approach. Diagnosed with breast cancer? There was a treatment for that. Diagnosed for prostate cancer? There was a different treatment for that, too. But now we know that there are different variants of breast cancer—different variants of prostate cancer, brain cancer, head and neck cancer, and the list goes on for most cancers.

Sometimes, one type of cancer can share identical or very similar growth mechanisms with a totally different cancer type. For example, my rare salivary duct cancer has a few close similarities to invasive ductal breast cancer and some similar characteristics to prostate cancer, as

Cynthia and I discovered in our research. In fact, every single cancer type has its own set of variants, and because each variation has its own unique mechanisms of action to drive its growth, knowing how to manipulate those mechanisms is the key to starving your cancer of the fuel it needs to grow. We found that to be true in my case after we discovered that a specific hormone was driving the growth of my cancer. The theory is that if one knows what drives the growth of the cancer, one can then begin to scour the planet for any reports involving drugs that serve to target the same mutations. If a targetable mutation was found and there was a drug somewhere in the world, then there was some hope that my life could be extended.

It was time for my follow-up appointment with Dr. Siu to discuss treatment. Cynthia and I knew that I would be offered the usual head and neck systemic treatment, usually involving platinum-based chemotherapy like Cisplatin, Carboplatin, and related derivatives. But with all of the research we had just done, Cynthia and I had a very different approach that we needed to discuss with Dr. Siu.

The appointment began as usual. We were brought into an exam/consultation room through one door and waited for Dr. Siu to enter the room from a door on the opposite side. It didn't take long before a confident Dr. Siu emerged with some papers in hand. Not knowing of our strategy, Dr. Siu began the appointment the same way I imagine she had done with countless other patients before me. The paperwork she had was to help me understand the chemotherapy she was about to prescribe. Dr. Siu's objective was obvious—she wanted to do anything she could to help—but my rare cancer (and the fact that it had already spread) presented a major obstacle for her. All she had to offer was the chemotherapy; however, Cynthia and I knew it wasn't enough.

When Dr. Siu was done speaking about the chemotherapy, I gathered my courage and suggested to one of the leading cancer experts in the world that I wanted to try something different. I explained that our research focused on the androgen-receptor positive feature of my tumour and that other people from around the world were experiencing significant benefits from androgen-deprivation therapy. I explained that not only were some people experiencing remission from the therapy, but the *durability* of the remission persisted far longer than any other treatment for metastatic salivary duct carcinoma. I knew that my word wasn't going to be enough, and that's why we brought with us the peer-reviewed reports in support of my requested treatment approach.

With hundreds of peer-reviewed journals being published internationally every day, it is impossible for any doctor to keep up with that volume of research—and impractical to expect of them. So we helped Dr. Siu by showing her various reports that supported my requested approach to treatment—that being androgen-deprivation therapy. Cynthia and I made the case very well, but we knew we didn't have to do all the work in convincing Dr. Siu. We knew the research would speak for itself.

It didn't take long before Dr. Siu accepted. She would withhold the chemotherapy in favor of androgen-deprivation therapy. But first, there was a practical problem to solve. The Princess Margarete Cancer Centre had not previously treated any salivary duct carcinoma patient with hormone-based therapy. I was told I was the first salivary duct carcinoma patient to be transferred to the prostate cancer clinic for treatment with androgen-deprivation therapy.

As a salvage attempt to survive my cancer, we went ahead with this treatment approach that would starve my tumour of the hormones it needed to grow—even though it had already spread to other parts of my body.

Like us, Dr. Siu and the specialists at the prostate cancer clinic recognized that there was nothing left to lose. I was 47 and was just told that my cancer was terminal. I was still young and had a budding family with kids at the ages of twelve and nine. Cynthia and I had already endured our own respective marriages and subsequent divorces; this was our time to continue discovering the depth and breadth of our love. I was going to do everything in my power to live for as long as I could. I had already lost precious time.

Even with the incredible amount of research we were doing and the positive aura we carried around with us, we never let go of reality and the very real possibility that this treatment may not work. I consulted with legal and financial professionals such that my will could be updated to create a cushion for my kids to land on as they mourned the loss of their dad at such young ages. I wondered which family members and friends would rise to the occasion to help guide my children after their loss. If cancer was going to be my downfall, it would *not* be the downfall of my family, as much as I could control.

The truth is, no amount of time, no amount of life experience can prepare you for this. It was all too much. There is never any time to waste, but you only ever realize that when it is almost too late.

Three months after beginning the hormone-based androgen-deprivation therapy, the moment of truth was upon us: it was time for the follow-up CT scan of my chest. As many cancer patients know, the lead-up to imaging scans can be very anxiety-provoking. Being treated at a progressive cancer centre meant that I was accustomed to receiving the results of all my tests via the patient portal. So when I received the email indicating that my CT report was available, I anxiously logged into the patient portal and read the result.

The CT scan showed that the tumours had dramatically reduced in size. It appeared as though all the positive things Cynthia and I had uncovered in our research were now benefiting me. It was my first indication that I may live longer than the sobering statistics suggested.

While this was an incredible moment to celebrate, my unrelenting fear eclipsed the possibility of a longer life. I continued to feel that the terminal nature of my cancer would not only *terminate* my life but also serve as an emotional impediment in the lives of my children, family, friends, and my beloved Cynthia.

Despite the shrinking tumours due to the hormone treatment, I was still buzzing with desperation, and panic was constantly coursing through me. The gravity of the situation blocked my access to the emotional tools I needed desperately to rely on. Those handmade emotional tools I had accumulated and used through my 25-year cancer journey were now out of my own reach. I needed help, and I needed it fast.

Chapter 20 Notes

_____

_____

_____

_____

_____

_____

_____

_____

_____

_____

_____

_____

_____

_____

CHAPTER 21

TREATING A RARE CANCER

There is no strict, universally agreed-upon definition of "rare cancer." Experts have different thresholds for what precisely qualifies a cancer as "rare." Some say the maximum threshold is two diagnoses in every 100,000 people each year, while others cite fewer than six in 100,000. According to the National Cancer Institute, rare cancers are those that occur in fewer than 15 out of 100,000 people each year—and my research has led me to adopt this 15-in-100,000 figure as a general rule.[1]

Within the cancer community, oncologists often refer to and rely on the American Surveillance, Epidemiology, and End Results (SEER) Program as a reference to help them better understand the rates, trends, and outcomes of individual cancers across a range of criteria, such as race, gender, age, geography, and more. The SEER program has been collecting data since 1975 and is an authoritative source of data on cancer incidence and mortality in the United States.[2] SEER collects and publishes cancer data from a set of 17 population-based regional cancer registries throughout the United States. The information from the database helps in many areas of oncology, including decision-making on where research must be focused to address the frequency and mortality of cancers over time.

Decisions regarding the direction of cancer research are critical. As you might expect, there is generally a direct relationship between the incidence of a specific cancer and the research dollars assigned to address those affected by it. For example, because breast cancer is so pervasive, the amount of research (and fundraising) assigned to address the disease is proportionally large compared to other cancers. This is great news for patients with many non-rare cancers. However, the story changes—and not in a good way—for those of us with the unfortunate luck of developing a rare cancer—people like me and, perhaps, you.

While each individual rare cancer is, in and of itself, rare (affecting fewer than 15 people per 100,000), the total number of rare cancer cases worldwide makes up approximately 22 percent of cancers diagnosed each year.[3] This means that one in five people diagnosed with cancer has a rare type.

According to SEER, my cancer type, salivary duct carcinoma, has an incidence rate of approximately 1 per 100,000. And as you would expect, the research effort assigned to address this cancer type is, at best, scant. That's not to say that there is zero research; it's just that locating data —*any* data that contain statistically meaningful results from anywhere in the world—is extremely difficult. With very few patients affected by these rare cancers, just assembling enough patients within a single study is almost impossible—so it's uncommon to draw any meaningful or statistically significant results.

So, what's the solution? Well, as it turns out, there are several options to help fill this huge gap, addressing the vast research disparity between rare cancers and their more common, ugly cousins.

One option relies on the fact that many rare cancers share similar characteristics with common cancers. For example, salivary duct carcinoma and invasive ductal breast cancer share some features. Therefore, some of the valuable research found within the domain of breast cancer can sometimes be applied to salivary duct carcinoma patients.

Similarly, some of the main growth drivers of salivary duct carcinoma are the hormones that belong to the androgen family, which are also found to drive the growth of prostate cancers. At some point in the recent past, an astute researcher first thought to apply the principles of androgen deprivation therapy to salivary duct carcinoma patients in a very small study, which helped some patients live longer than they otherwise would have. So, if prostate cancer research did not reveal androgen receptor activation in some patients, it's likely that Cynthia and I would not have stumbled upon this treatment as an option for me.

While there is some measure of success within the rare cancer community, currently, it is more the exception than the rule. Rare cancer research generally remains stymied due to a lack of funding.[4] Research efforts generally follow the money, and unfortunately, there is little financial incentive for mainstream researchers to invest their time in studying rare cancers when the return on their investment would be low. In 2018, the top three cancers funded by the National Cancer Institute received close to $1.2 billion in funding, while salivary gland cancer received a measly $625,300—or 0.05% (one-half of one percent) of that amount.[5]

So, what can be done? Enter TargetCancer Foundation: https://www.targetcancerfoundation.org

TargetCancer Foundation is a beacon of hope for patients and families affected by rare cancers. Their mission is to promote the development of lifesaving treatment protocols for rare cancers. They achieve this by directly supporting initiatives at the forefront of cancer treatment through funding innovative research, fostering collaborations, and raising awareness among scientists, clinicians, and patients.

As with so many successful initiatives advancing to create meaningful change, TargetCancer Foundation was created by an individual desperate for effective treatment options for his rare cancer. At the age of 38, Paul Poth was diagnosed with a rare cancer called cholangiocarcinoma—a notoriously deadly cancer that conducts itself with particularly swift efficiency. With no available standard of care, the best treatment options were those found in other cancer treatment protocols. Unfortunately, the outcome for Paul was as predictable as were the effects of the harsh chemotherapy he endured. Prior to Paul's untimely passing in 2009, he began TargetCancer Foundation with the view of raising funds as quickly as possible in support of the most innovative and promising research into otherwise ignored rare cancers.

To honour Paul's vision, his wife Kristen and brother-in-law Jim Palma have since developed TargetCancer Foundation into a legitimate bastion of hope for those affected with rare cancers. Through their vast network of relationships with like-minded people within the greater cancer research community, Paul's vision is slowly coming into focus.

One of the key challenges with rare cancers is that many patients are excluded from clinical trials. To address this, TargetCancer Foundation has expanded its impact through a prospective clinical trial called TCF-001 TRACK (Target Rare Cancer Knowledge) which seeks to enrol 400 patients with rare cancers or cancer of unknown primary.

TRACK provides participating rare cancer patients and their physicians with personalized, actionable information to potentially inform treatment, as well as recommendations from an expert panel of rare cancer clinicians and scientists. At the same time, TRACK generates critical genomic data to drive a better understanding of often overlooked rare cancers. Through an innovative remote consenting process, patients can fully consent and enrol in the TRACK study from their home without travelling to a clinical trial site.

If you or a loved one are facing a rare cancer, you would be wise to consider reaching out to TargetCancer Foundation. At the time of the publication of this book, TRACK can only enrol patients from the United States; however, by the time you are reading this, those guidelines may have changed—or there could be another clinical trial, or they may have entered into agreements with partners in Canada or other countries. Regardless, TargetCancer Foundation is a light that shines further and brighter each day for those with rare cancers.

More information on TRACK and TargetCancer Foundation can be found at their website https://www.targetcancerfoundation.org/. You'll find this and other resources listed in Appendix C of the book for your convenience.

Chapter 21 Notes

_____

_____

_____

_____

_____

_____

_____

_____

_____

_____

_____

_____

_____

_____

CHAPTER 22

TURNING INWARD

To fully appreciate what it takes to care for a cancer patient, one must understand that the care is comprehensive. It's not one doctor or caregiver who tends to the patient; it isn't even one person who fights the cancer. It is an entire team, a *community* that takes on the burden and acts as a support structure for the patient—and it's not *just* the cancer itself that is treated. My community was essential for my survival—physically, and emotionally.

Throughout my journey, I made sure to try to know the names of every doctor, resident, nurse, technician, pharmacist, clerk, and student who had a hand in my treatment and ongoing care. I even went as far as to write them down so as not to forget. In total, there were over 30 medical professionals who took time out of their lives to ensure that I kept mine for as long as possible.

As you now know, when I was first diagnosed with my salivary duct cancer in 2016, most people in my life only knew of my cancer and radiation treatments, but only Cynthia and I knew of its terminal nature. But everyone else in my life knew of my cancer and treatments. I was not doing well at all. While I had countless friends and family members—most specifically, my parents, who continued to offer me their support in any way they could—I needed to step out of the limelight and become unavailable. I needed to turn inward.

I would be remiss if I didn't share this side of the cancer experience. This is not just my experience but the experience of many cancer patients I've met. It is as ugly as it is true: some people feel the need to turn their backs on a friend or family member who has cancer.

Phone calls stop. Emails stop. Text messages stop. All contact stops. The relationship doesn't necessarily end; however, it shifts to a place where a full recovery is no longer possible.

Unfortunately, many of the relationships I held dear suffered on account of my need to turn inward after my terminal diagnosis. It gives me no pleasure to speak of this truth, but it does offer me some relief to memorialize it in my book with the view of helping others. To those people in my sphere who made this decision, who decided to make my cancer about them, I say, "Thank you." Thank you for a relationship I continue to look back on with fondness. Thank you for the good times, the laughs, and the rich experiences we shared together. And thank you for showing me your true colours in my time of need.

Your actions allowed me to focus my precious time on the people who stepped up in support of my needs. I regret that you couldn't see or support that my time of need meant I needed to turn inward—that after a lifetime of being a people pleaser, an always-available person, turning inward was something I needed to do for myself. I'm sorry you found this offensive. With the extra time you have to live beyond the all-but-certainty of my early death, I hope you can learn from your mistreatment of me. And finally, when it is your time to consider your own imminent death, I hope that you are treated with more dignity and care than you offered me.

To all the other people in my life who offered their unconditional love and support, I can only hope to make up for lost time. While I will not apologize for needing to focus exclusively on survival, thereby becoming unavailable to family and friends, they all need to know that their love and support were key factors in helping me hold on to my motivation to survive. As I continue to survive and thrive in my current state of remission, I will do my best to show by my actions and words how grateful I am for the support of my loved ones and close friends through the most difficult challenge I have ever faced.

Two people must be singled out and acknowledged. If not for them, I truly believe that my life would have ended over the course of the last five years.

The first is my beloved Cynthia. In 2016, when it became clear that I was deathly ill, she stopped working in order to be fully available to me. Although her ever-changing roles varied from day-to-day, her love and support were as reliable as one could hope for. She would sit stoically by my side at every hospital appointment; she was my travel companion to New York and Houston for second and third opinions; she would consistently and patiently listen to my initial (and then repeated) negativity. And when I was done ranting, Cynthia would offer me a balanced perspective with her unyielding positivity.

Despite dealing with these challenges and the same overwhelming sense of doom I myself faced, Cynthia never gave up. She remained positive every day. This proved to be one of the keys to my own eventual positivity. When I couldn't guide myself through the flames of certain death, she took control and led me to a clearing where I could escape the scorching heat. It was an impossible task, but she did it out of love. I am the luckiest person alive to not only have met Cynthia but to have her love me. This is more of a blessing than my continued survival.

The second person worthy of specific individual gratitude is Dr. Madline Li at the Princess Margaret Cancer Centre. To balance my physical care with my emotional wellbeing, I was referred to the Psychosocial Oncology Clinic for the purpose of receiving psychological supportive care in 2016.

From the Fall of 2016 to early 2020, I was fortunate to work closely and frequently with Dr. Li—a remarkable woman in her own right—who took me under her capable wing and helped me through a very dark and deep depression. At the conclusion of our first meeting together, her parting words helped me realize that not all hope was lost.

"I think we can do some really good work together."

For the uninitiated, the value of cancer's psychological impact may not be immediately obvious. One might think that cancer is "difficult" but not necessarily difficult to the point that professional psychological support would be of value. While this may be the case for some, it is the opposite for others.

Some people find it difficult to talk about, much less examine their emotions—particularly those emotions that revolve around existential issues. I am not one of them. I have always felt that a deep connection with one's emotions has a direct impact on one's general wellbeing and one's ability to overcome adversity. So, for me, having just been diagnosed with terminal cancer and being forced to address my mortality, attending to my emotions in a deep way was a necessary step if I was to have any chance of emotional survival.

Emotional survival in the context of a terminal cancer diagnosis is a very important concept that took me quite some time to get my head around. The goal is to recognize and appreciate that while my body was about to be overrun with an irreversible disease I had no control over, I could learn how to emotionally survive and thrive from this experience—even in the face of death. But how? How can one survive and then thrive emotionally when they know that their cancer is terminal, that their untimely death is fast approaching? Enter Dr. Li.

When I had my heart attack in May of 2013, I vividly recall those tense moments in the cardiac catheterization suite, where the interventional cardiologists were attempting to install stents that would open up the blockages in my heart. I was totally awake and aware during the entire procedure. I watched on four monitors how they threaded a very thin catheter through an artery in my wrist up towards my shoulder and then directly to my heart, where they deployed the stents. These doctors saved my life. When the procedure was done, I was in utter shock of what they had just done for me and my family. I cannot overstate the profound effect their ability to unblock my coronary arteries had on me.

Similar to a cardiologist, Dr. Li's specialty is to identify *emotional* blockages and use *emotional* stenting techniques to provide a patient with relief. This work can not be done in the 45 minutes it took to open up the blockages in my heart; rather, the work that Dr. Li and I undertook spanned a three-year period.

During cardiac catheterization, I passively lay there while the cardiologists performed their task. In contrast, the success of Dr. Li's work was dependent on her skill of carefully threading her probe into my emotions in concert with my ability to actively and willingly engage in the process. There was active work to do—and lots of it.

Together, Dr. Li and I explored many aspects of my life across the decades. And as you now know, my decades overflowed with remarkable events that served to highlight important areas to be explored further. Unfortunately, my life was not wanting for difficult content... but the flip side was that the unsavoury events of my life helped Dr. Li to target the emotional blockages that needed to be cleared.

Dr. Li approached this work with the utmost professionalism and sensitivity. She recognized that I was driven to do my best to physically survive and that I was committed to addressing my emotions as healthily as possible, given my distressing circumstances.

Despite our combined commitment to succeed, there was no question I was experiencing severe emotional symptoms consistent with major depression. I was 47 years old with two young children of my own and living parents who had already buried my brother. My life was coming to an end—or so I thought—and I had just met Cynthia three years earlier. I saw Cynthia's heart breaking before my eyes. She had anticipatory anxiety about my deteriorating health and likely death. So, yeah—I had plenty to be depressed about.

The thick cloud of my depression prevented me from seeing the benefit of sharing intimate details of my medical issues with family and friends. Why was I not able to disclose to my family and friends that my cancer was indeed terminal? Why did it affect my active participation in ongoing relationships and activities with the people closest to me? I feel that the answers are elusive because the existential nature of these questions is rarely (if ever) addressed early in life when the carefree years dominate. Dr. Li sympathized and offered multiple approaches to help. She needed my mental health to be as good as possible if I had any chance of opening up emotional blockages and emotionally surviving this catastrophe.

In addition to our regularly scheduled sessions, Dr. Li prescribed numerous medications to help break through the thick cloud of paralyzing depression. For the most part, these medications helped—but only to a degree. Despite her effort, my compliance, and my commitment to my own betterment, I still was unable to see the value in being publically forthcoming about the nature of my terminal illness—and after trying different combinations of medications, I was still extremely depressed. In professional circles, they call this "treatment-resistant depression."

But Dr. Li was not prepared to give up on me. She was determined to help me, and that's when she proposed something new—something that was showing promise for treatment-resistant depression. She name-dropped a medication that had been around for many years but was now being repurposed for treatment-resistant depression. This drug was ketamine.

Approved in 1970, ketamine was primarily used by anesthesiologists when beginning and maintaining anaesthesia in the operating room. It was also used in veterinary medicine, specifically for dogs and horses that required sedation. Health professionals see value in ketamine because, in addition to its sedating properties, it also preserves breathing and airway reflexes, along with stimulating heart function and increasing blood pressure. Unfortunately, ketamine is also used as a recreational street drug, giving it a bad reputation. It's a highly controlled drug for this reason, and only a few pharmacies in Toronto were able to compound it in the form and concentration Dr. Li needed. If you want to get weird looks from a pharmacist, walk into a pharmacy with a prescription for ketamine....

It only took a few doses of ketamine for me to find the relief I had been yearning for. For the first time, it was as if the fog of death had cleared, and I was able to see beyond my negative health circumstances. A true breakthrough was being unearthed.

It didn't take long before my emotions were in the normal zone, and I was able to be more forthcoming about my health circumstances with my loved ones. As you may appreciate, it was by no means easy to tell the people I care about the most that I have terminal cancer, but I did it. And this book, in and of itself, is a testament to the work that Dr. Li and I did together. I was happy to be her mini-Frankenstein. I can only hope that should you need emotional support, you have access to your own Dr. Li, wherever you may live.

As I mentioned at the beginning of this chapter, my survival would not have been possible without the incredible team of people who supported me physically *and* emotionally—in particular, Cynthia and Dr. Li. And your survival, if you ever find yourself in a similar situation, would not be possible without the help and support of the team *you* create and *your* commitment to succeed for as long as possible.

Just as I have found time in my struggle to thank those who helped me along the way, I urge you to do the same. Genuine appreciation and gratitude will go a long way in creating a steady stream of motivation for you to continue to fight, survive, and thrive.

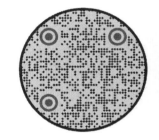

I'd like to share with you one very important additional piece of my coping puzzle that has worked miracles for me. In 2017, my daughter, Hila, was nine years old. She has a beautiful singing voice, and she recorded a song for me from one of our favourite musicals, *In the Heights*, written by Lin-Manuel Miranda. The song is titled "Breathe," and I listened to it each day—sometimes more than once each day. And as a special bonus for you, I've included that recording here. Simply scan the QR code with your mobile device to listen.

Chapter 22 Notes

_____

_____

_____

_____

_____

_____

_____

_____

_____

_____

_____

_____

_____

_____

_____

_____

CHAPTER 23

PLAYING THE GAME TO WIN

After experiencing the trials and challenges that come with a health crisis such as a rare, terminal cancer, a few things have become clear to me. Most importantly, I have discovered what is truly important in my life and what I need to let go of—not only to be happy that I've survived so far, but to thrive and embrace these final years as the best part of my life.

One such example of this is the importance of being passionate about the things in your life. This includes the obvious choices and subjects, such as family, health, your job, and your friends. However, what stood out to me—and what helped me find the emotional strength to push through this terminal cancer diagnoses and other health issues—was that I needed to be passionate about something that had *no connection* to my illness at all. I needed to find enjoyment in something, a hobby completely removed from the medical field. In doing so, in finding this outlet, I was able to take a break from being bombarded with treatments, negative thoughts, and medical jargon to clear my mind and find my motivation.

For me, this outlet was the game of backgammon.

I had played the game growing up, and it had quickly turned into a favourite pastime for me and the people I am still lucky enough to call my close friends.

I still remember, quite clearly and very fondly, all of us getting together to have multiple backgammon games going at the same time. Those game nights were serious business, and the competition was fierce. Not only did we all jockey to be the best, but we would often bet on who would buy dinner or financially contribute in some other way to ensure that the loser of the night would feel the sting of their defeat. I've often been asked why I am as competitive as I am and how I came to be so, and I must attribute it, with absolute certainty, to those nights of playing backgammon with my friends as a young man.

The games would go on until all hours of the night, even into the wee hours of the morning, and would include many of the same events and traditions. For one, the loser of the night would always ask to play for double or nothing. "Just one more game" would be the consistent refrain. For the person who was up in their winnings for the night, it was as customary as it was courteous to accept the challenge to play for double or nothing. At best, the money would double, and at worst, you were a good friend. Win or lose, we would always be drawn together again to play more and have fun. Those were some of my best life memories. These guys have no idea the positive impact their friendships, all of them, had on me.

And fun it was. Amazing, actually. However, as time went by, our lives began naturally to change and grow. Those nights full of gameplay and friendly yet competitive gambling became less and less frequent. Life happened, and that was a good thing. Some of us got married and had kids; still others moved away, looking for love because they had exhausted all the available candidates in Montreal. But it didn't matter because we stayed in very close contact, and the vast majority of these friendships are as strong today as they ever were—just with a little more grey hair, which is a great thing.

Fast forward 30 years: I have two beautiful teenage kids. I've survived an initial cancer diagnosis at age 21, a heart attack at 43, and a second (and terminal) cancer diagnosis at 46—now trying to live what is left of my life amidst a global pandemic. I began to yearn for the sort of camaraderie and happiness I once enjoyed during those competitive nights of my youth.

What the heck was I supposed to do? Still undergoing health issues— paired with the fact that the entire world seemed to have shut down for almost two years—it was hard for anyone to find an escape from the stresses of life. Still, I was resolved to return to the game of backgammon.

In 2020, during the pandemic, I joined the United States Backgammon Federation (USBGF) with the goal of reigniting the backgammon hobby I'd given up 30 years earlier in exchange for my career and raising my two children. But due to global circumstances combined with how the play of the game had evolved over the years, my return to backgammon was slightly complicated.

While playing backgammon face-to-face with a traditional backgammon board was the preferred way to play, the COVID-19 pandemic created opportunities for online backgammon players via a number of virtual backgammon websites. This made it very convenient to find a player anywhere in the world 24/7. During the lockdown, it seemed that online backgammon was going to be the best (and only) way I could re-enter the world I had left so many years earlier.

I quickly understood that during my 30 year hiatus, there had been big advancements in game analysis using artificial intelligence and neural networks, which changed the concept of what it means to "win" a game of backgammon. When I was younger, the winner was the first opponent who bore off their 15 checkers, but nowadays, world renowned online backgammon destinations define a *true* win to now include the player who *made the fewest mistakes* in addition to bearing off their checkers first.

In the traditional game, when one player won, it was simply assumed they had played more skillfully than the loser. But it was theoretically (and arguably, practically) impossible for anyone to *truly* know *how* they won: what moves directly led to their victory and how their moves compared to those of their opponents. Now, with the advent of online backgammon, these questions can be answered.

At the end of each online match, players can use readily available software to assess each move of every game, showing the player whether they made the best move—and, if not, what the best move *should* have been. This software, called Extreme Gammon, is now used by the world's best backgammon players to help them train.

These advancements in the game have created much more competitive gameplay, requiring a much more strategic mind. With each roll of the dice, as each player moves their checkers to the best of their skill, the software calculates in real time what the odds are of winning that game. Effectively, the software calculates the odds of winning or losing at any given point during that game or match.

One day, in late August 2020, just a few days prior to one of my follow-up CT scans, I was playing a game of online backgammon against an opponent halfway across the world. In this game, I was certain I had no possible chance of winning. It would have taken a string of miracles to not lose the game. Not to belabour the climax, suffice it to say, I ended up winning in spite of the odds.

I know to most, it's just a game, and it's not wrong to think that way. But for me, this win—the probability of which dictated that it should not have happened—against the looming backdrop of my upcoming CT scan was impossible to ignore. After the game, I downloaded all the moves. In an instant, the software told me that at my worst position of the game, I had a 2.3 percent chance of winning.

At that moment, everything became clear.

Despite the awful odds that come with a terminal cancer diagnosis—or any severe and life-threatening illness—one needs to understand that there is always room for hope—that some success can be found in the darkness of seemingly certain failure.

Failure is never 100 percent certain; there is always a statistical possibility of success.

(Cynthia recorded the moment that I won this game. As an extra special bonus, I'm including that brief video here so you can see my reaction, in real time, for yourself. Just scan the QR code on your mobile device.)

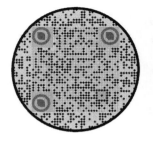

I have since gathered the courage to place myself in competitive tournament play within the United States Backgammon Federation, going up against some of the best players in the world. Despite my abysmal odds and the amateur status that I entered the tournament with, I have won four tournaments and placed second in several others.

More important than winning money in these tournaments or seeing my name published is that the message of continued survival despite horrible odds seems to be persisting for me. This was the same message Cynthia had been telling me all along, but this time in a different form. Even if it seems that you don't have a chance to survive, think again, because you do. Fight *hard*, make wise decisions, and never give up hope.

Being able to escape to a world entirely outside of the medical one, I was able not only to find calm and repose but able to seize my own motivation and life lessons. This is extremely profound because it helped me further appreciate that my remission isn't just about surviving. Remission from terminal cancer gives me pause to carefully consider the meaning of life: to think carefully about what is truly important and what isn't; to take stock in those relationships that are meaningful, in both directions; to make the time to live with and love those that matter the most; and—even though it's hard and sad—to have the opportunity to say thank you and good-bye to people who mean the most to me.

It's utterly amazing that, of all things, it was my love for the game of backgammon and my competitive nature that opened the door to a deep level of understanding I never knew existed. Playing the game of backgammon showed me just how real the possibility of success is when you play the game to win. So, I encourage you to go find your own door. It's there—all you have to do is find it, open it, and then walk through.

Chapter 23 Notes

_____

_____

_____

_____

_____

_____

_____

_____

_____

_____

_____

_____

_____

_____

CHAPTER 24

UNDERSTANDING REMISSION

T he goal of every cancer treatment and the hope of everyone faced with cancer is simple: remission. It certainly was my goal, and it is currently the state in which I live my life to this day. But what *is* remission? How does it happen? And how can you increase your odds of achieving it?

When we talk about cancer, some of the terms we use are scientific, while others are phrases adopted over time by laypeople and experts to describe their experiences. As much as possible, I have tried throughout the book to use the correct terms to describe recoveries and treatments. Still, sometimes there may be overlap between a scientific term and the lived experience of a cancer survivor. In any case, the gist of the matter is the same: living longer, getting better, and becoming cancer-free.

Remission specifically is a tricky and convoluted topic to fully understand. *Remission* means a reduction in the signs and symptoms of your cancer. This reduction can be complete or partial. In complete remission, all the signs and symptoms of the cancer are gone; in partial remission, only some of the signs and symptoms have disappeared. Moreover, it is not the sudden loss of a symptom that is considered remission; it is, rather, a *sustained* lack of symptoms. Most doctors consider anyone who has stayed in complete remission for up to five years to be cured.[1] Remission is not a cure, but it is the first step towards living cancer-free.

Because remission is such a vague term, others terms are used to help specify what a cancer patient may be going through on their road to full recovery.

Regression[2]

Although the term remission is commonly used to mean being free of any kind of cancer signs and symptoms, remission *technically* refers to cancers of the blood with no tumour. Technically, when cancer with a solid tumour shrinks or disappears, it is known as *regression*.

Spontaneous Remission

Spontaneous remission is defined as the partial or total disappearance of the signs and symptoms of cancer in the absence of treatment or in the presence of a treatment not considered sufficient to create such an effect on the cancer. In other words, it is the condition of attaining remission without receiving adequate conventional therapies. It is also used to describe remission in patients who fail to respond to conventional treatments but go on to achieve remission.

Spontaneous Regression

Spontaneous regression means the same thing as spontaneous remission, but the term is reserved for solid tumours (not for blood cancers).

Radical Remission

Radical remission is a term popularized by Dr. Kelly Turner in her book by the same name. In the book, she defines radical remission as "any cancer remission that is statistically unexpected, and those statistics vary depending on the cancer type, stage, and medical treatment received."[3]

Exceptional Survivors

An exceptional survivor of cancer is an individual who has outlived actuarial predictions for their form of cancer or one who experiences a complete disappearance of the signs and symptoms. Such people have also been described as having a remarkable recovery.

Previously, exceptional survivors were regarded as irrelevant outliers, but now scientists are making efforts to study their lives for clues to help others achieve sustained survivorship.

Five-Year Survival Rate

The National Cancer Institute defines the five-year survival rate as the percentage of people in a study or treatment group who are alive five years after they were diagnosed with, or started treatment for, a disease such as cancer.[4]

Doctors often use the five-year survival rate to measure how well a person is likely to respond to cancer treatments and to discuss the natural course the cancer is expected to take.

Cure

There are a few reasons the term "cure" is used with caution when discussing cancer.

First, cancer is not one disease but a term used to describe over 200 different conditions with similar properties that can affect almost any group of cells in the body. And while many cancers are well understood and controlled, other cancers, particularly rare cancers, remain not well understood. For example, while Hodgkin's disease is one form of cancer that can generally be well controlled, pancreatic cancer, as an example, is one that remains elusive and very difficult to control. In my case, my Hodgkin's disease was considered "cured" because, after 5 years, there was no detectable cancer. However, fast forward 25 years, and my metastatic salivary duct carcinoma is one cancer with abysmal 5-year survival rates.

Second, it can be hard to tell if the cancer is completely gone or if the disappearance of signs and symptoms is temporary. For these reasons, scientists are careful not to gratuitously use the word "cure," preferring instead to speak in terms of remission or regression.

Just as cancer is a process, remission is one, as well. Just as there is no cure, there is no one version or kind of remission. Being in remission is being in a continuous state of having no cancerous symptoms, signs, or detectable cancer cells or tumour.

There is no "survived" when it comes to conquering cancer—there is only *surviving*. You are always in the present; you are always surviving and thriving. Your survival is never complete or done.

And why should it be? You will have worked hard to get to the point of remission and surviving. Embrace this part and live it for as long as you can.

Chapter 24 Notes

_____

_____

_____

_____

_____

_____

_____

_____

_____

_____

_____

_____

_____

_____

_____

_____

CHAPTER 25

HINDSIGHT IS ALWAYS 20/20

The sheer number of thoughts that run through your mind when you undergo a trauma can make the entire experience a blur. Days, months, and even years pass incredibly fast, yet, at the same time, you feel as though you are at a standstill. Only after you have completely gone through the trauma—or at least when you are coming to the end—do you begin to see things more clearly. Events and experiences that happened during your hardest times come back to you as though they are parts of a movie you have never seen or that you have forgotten.

In this way, you remember your journey, struggles, challenges, and eventual successes much differently than you viewed them when they were happening. For me, once I was in my state of remission, I began to see symbols, metaphors, and connections between past times in my life and my present. One of the most notable symbolic connections came to me as a sort of emotional epiphany when I was watching a Broadway performance of *The Lion King*.

The repetition of the melody in "The Circle of Life" brought me back to one of the most terrifying days of my past. I was transported through time to come face to face with the day I was told I had a lump in my chest and clavicle area that was to be tested for cancerous cells.

On that day, I was headed to my geology class at Concordia University in Montreal. The building housing this class was of a particularly interesting shape. It was a circular building which was different from the normal shaped buildings on campus. The rounded shape of this building juxtaposed against the standard brick architecture of the rest of the university made it stand out.

It wasn't until this moment, watching an emotional song and dance scene in *The Lion King*, that I realized the symbolism of this round building. Life is full of cycles that begin, progress, end, and then repeat themselves over and over. Even life itself is a circle in its structure, beginning with birth, progressing through different challenges and experiences, and ending with death, only to then begin again with new life.

The round building marked a time when my life began a new cycle of challenges and experiences. Although I could not see it at the time, the building was there to show me that, although I was about to face challenging times, the cycle of life would bring me back to peace and calm eventually. It was only when I sat in my seat in a New York theatre with my two children to watch a live performance of *The Lion King* that I realized just how true and reliable these cycles of life are. During that Broadway performance, flanked by my children, the emotions just flooded in.

Challenges give way to success; times of battle and wars give way to times of peace; illness gives way to health. This return to the good in our lives is something we must remember, especially in times of illness, pain, and struggle. Too many of us only pay attention when good times are crowded out by negative experiences.

Life is not linear or one-directional. It is not the *line* of life. It is the *circle* of life.

Chapter 25 Notes

_____

_____

_____

_____

_____

_____

_____

_____

_____

_____

_____

_____

_____

_____

Some Final Thoughts
(For the Book, That Is...)

The evolution of cancer care and scientific advancement is such that if you have to get cancer and if you want to live with it, now is the optimal time in medical history for you to have the best chances of achieving remission, radical or otherwise.

All the strategies and concepts that I suggest you attempt to acquire a state of remission are predicated on your will to live and your drive to survive. The elements that contribute to one's will to live are generally specific to the person, varying from one individual to the next and based on the circumstances of one's life. In my case, I could identify three major elements that fuelled my will to live:

- I wanted my children to have access to their father for as long as possible, particularly during their formative years.
- I did not want to die before my parents, thereby shielding them from the unrelenting turmoil of the loss of a second child.
- I wanted to continue experiencing the refreshing effervescence of my love with Cynthia as it deepened over time.

As of the publication of this book in early 2022, I will have enjoyed five years of radical remission from a cancer that should have,statistically, taken my life in 2018. That I have had this opportunity, this time—it has been and continues to be a blessing. As amazing as that is (and it's pretty f'ing amazing), while I continue to enjoy more of life, the excitement stops there.

Some people mistakenly believe that once they achieve a state of radical remission, they are cured of the disease. This is most often not the case. If one is lucky enough to achieve a state of radical remission, one must be careful to avoid being pulled into the trap of hubris. Falsely equating remission with a cure is foolish and will most likely lead to profound disappointment.

My suggestion is simple: if given the opportunity to live on borrowed time, having relied on the principles I have laid out within these pages, know well that your cancer is likely in a state of dormancy or otherwise quietly figuring out a way around your current treatment. Remember that your cancer has one goal—*SURVIVAL*—and that goal competes directly with *your* goal to survive.

The day will most likely come when your cancer has either grown to a level of detection or is causing you symptomatic discomfort. Either way, you will most likely be forced to re-examine your approach to your disease and consider the possibility of alternative treatment options for recurrent disease.

I am currently in the position where the durability of my remission is likely to soon fail, and I am therefore in active pursuit of more information around advances in diagnostic and treatment approaches for salivary duct carcinoma. I feel a proactive approach will be more effective in my attempt to achieve a possible second remission. I would therefore suggest that a proactive approach is likely one of your best options should you be lucky enough to contemplate a state of remission for a second time.

I hope, with the utmost sincerity, that my story and the information I've shared will assist you in your own journey. I hope you will appreciate that terminal disease in 2022 has another side—a side rich with life, love, and the opportunity to live beyond the statistics. Through my own experience, it is my strong belief that *you* can be that one in five. So, if you or a loved one is navigating the threat of cancer, even terminal cancer, I encourage you to embrace the roadmap to remission that has so greatly benefitted my family and me. If it could happen to me, it can happen to you, too.

I wish you much success. I hope that you or a loved one can enjoy the blessing and elation of having more time and the opportunity to live on the other side of terminal.

A Personal Request

I hope that you found my story and the things I did to position myself for remission to be helpful. If you feel that you gleaned some insight or inspiration, I'd like to request a quick favour. Please take a moment to leave me a thoughtful, honest review on Amazon. Reviews can make a huge difference in helping others discover my book.

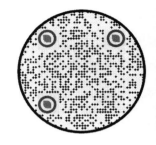

Scan the QR code or go to the book's product page at your preferred book retailer and look for the review section.

Appendix A

My Lifestyle Advice for Surviving Cancer

While the definitive cure for cancer continues to elude the medical community, it does seem closer than ever. Every day, scientists search for more effective methods to fight cancer, and as you learned in Chapter 14, promising new experimental treatments are being developed. And there are a variety of tools—presented in the form of lifestyle changes—that can provide you the best chance of successfully fighting the illness. We need to know what we can do to increase our chances of getting into and staying in remission.

Lifestyle changes are notoriously hard to make—especially when you are struggling and fighting for your life—but some who have been able to make certain changes to their lifestyle while fighting cancer have achieved excellent results. It is a good idea to know as many lifestyle changes associated with a positive outcome as possible if you want to increase your chance of being successful. In doing so, you will give yourself the best chance of adopting at least one positive change.

Some of the most popular lifestyle changes include:

- Food
- Dietary and herbal supplements
- Drinks
- Exercise
- Emotions
- Intuition
- Purpose

FOOD

Let thy food be thy medicine and thy medicine be thy food
    –Hippocrates

Food is vital for survival; this is not a secret. However, certain foods are healthier than others, and some foods even have cancer-fighting properties.

Nutritional science is one of the most rapidly evolving controversial disciplines. It has been nearly impossible for nutritionists and doctors to agree on which diet is the best for optimal health. That being said, throughout the years, scientists have agreed on some things when it comes to a healthy diet. In general, a Mediterranean diet is generally considered to be a healthy choice. This diet has been associated with better all-round health and is considered a good choice for most people.

The Mediterranean diet adopts the traditional food choices of people living in countries, like Spain, Greece, Italy, and France, bordering the Mediterranean Sea. This diet is typically high in vegetables, fruits, legumes, cereals, beans, nuts, grains, and fish. It also relies on unsaturated fats like olive oil. What's more, there is little to no intake of meat and dairy products.[1]

The Mediterranean diet is not the only choice. People have chosen other diets as part of their recovery plan with good results. Other diets you can consider are the ketogenic diet, the pescatarian diet, and the vegan/vegetarian diet.

It is important to note that, when it comes to food, it is a good idea to avoid overeating. Excessive calories cause more harm than good, leading to diseases such as obesity, which can not only work to complicate the fight against but also *lead* to cancer. While each of the abovementioned diets differs slightly from the other, they all avoid the consumption of excessive calories.

Whatever diet you choose, discuss your choice with your doctors and a nutritionist to make sure you give your body the fuel it needs and the best chance for recovery.

Beyond some specific diets you can follow, simply including foods that have cancer-fighting properties can help increase your chances of surviving the illness. Cancer-fighting foods include, but are not limited to, fruits and vegetables, nuts, fish, and even some spices and herbs.

Try not to be intimidated by the sheer amount of information surrounding what is healthy food and what isn't. Be sure to do your own research about what foods work best for you and discuss with your doctor and medical team which foods you should include in (and which foods you should take out of) your diet.

DRINKS

In time and with water, everything changes
  –Leonardo da Vinci

In a similar way as food affects our bodies, what we drink can have a huge impact, as well.

Most specifically, ensuring that you are drinking enough water and avoiding or eliminating other drinks like soda, alcohol, and sweetened beverages can bring about the largest health benefits and success. Nutritionists recommend at least eight glasses of water a day for everyone as it is vital for many processes in the body and helps flush out toxins.[2]

Many people attest to the benefits they experienced when they focused on drinking enough water every day while receiving cancer treatments. Water works wonders. Drink enough of it to help your body function optimally. Different kinds of teas, coffee, and juices can also work to build and support your body's immune system—that is, only when they are free from added sugars, chemicals, and additives.

EXERCISE

Good things come to those who sweat
  –Unknown

Exercise has been described as the silver bullet for a healthy life. As it turns out, exercise helps the body fight cancer, too. Studies show that exercise boosts your body's cancer-fighting abilities in many ways.[3]

The following is a laundry list of ways exercise can help increase your chances of surviving cancer. I say "laundry list" to underscore just how beneficial including exercise in your life can be.

- **Boosting immune system function.** Studies in mice showed that exercise reduces inflammation and makes the body hostile to cancer cells. The same changes are believed to happen in humans when they exercise.
- **Reducing your risk of certain side effects of medication,** such as nausea, fatigue, neuropathy, lymphedema, and osteoporosis. Many cancer treatments come with unwanted side effects. Exercise helps strengthen your body and minimize these conditions.
- **Preventing loss of muscle and building strength.** Exercise helps your muscles grow and get stronger. By exercising, you can prevent the typical muscle loss that occurs during an illness.
- **Improving body functions,** such as sleep and bowel

movements. Drugs, poor diet, and even anxiety can affect bodily functions, which can further worsen a bad mood and ill health. Exercise helps you sleep better and keeps you regular, too.

- **Mood-boosting.** Fighting cancer can be depressing. Exercise helps improve your mood and reduces your risk of depression, anxiety, and other mental health conditions.
- **Making your treatments more effective.** Exercise improves blood circulation and the removal of waste products, helping medications work better and helping you recover faster.
- **Improving your survival rate.** Scientists have shown that people who exercise during and after treatment for cancer have a higher survival rate than those who don't.
- **Preventing other chronic health conditions,** such as heart disease, hypertension, and diabetes. Fighting cancer doesn't make you immune from other diseases. However, regular exercise can help prevent or reduce them. A lifestyle that embraces regular exercise has been proven to prevent many chronic diseases.
- **Improving your balance and reducing your risk of falls and other injuries.** Exercise helps you stay agile and keep your balance, preventing falls and other injuries.
- **Preventing and reducing weight gain and obesity.** Weight gain and obesity have been associated with certain cancer medications as well as a sedentary lifestyle. Regular exercise will help you stay fit and keep your weight normal.

Adding exercise into your lifestyle can be a tricky change to make. After all, not everyone can go to the gym every day, nor is everyone able to do every type of exercise. There are many contributing factors to consider, ensuring the exercises you include in your routine are both beneficial and safe.

The type of exercise that is best for you will vary depending on:

- Your age.
- Your fitness levels.
- Treatments you are receiving.
- The type of cancer you are being treated for.
- Any health problems you are facing.
- Any side effects you may be experiencing.
- Your resources and environment.

You should discuss any major exercise changes with your medical team before you begin to ensure that the activity is safe and right for you. Additionally, you should start slow and increase the intensity as you improve to avoid injury.

There is no point in including exercise in your life if it will cause more harm than good.

EMOTIONS

Guard your heart with all diligence for out of it proceed the issues of life
    –King Soloman

Many cancer survivors have shared their experiences with recovery that involved dealing with and releasing negative emotions. This is a profoundly personal issue, but it is worth examining while you are on the journey to recovery.

In her comprehensive book about cancer survivors titled *Radical Remission*, Dr. Kelly Turner notes that emotional mastery is an essential ingredient for attaining remission in many patients.

Some of the emotional processes she discusses are:[4]

1. Releasing suppressed emotions.
2. Increasing positive emotions.
3. Embracing social support.
4. Deepening your spiritual connection.
5. Having a strong reason for living.

As with most suggestions to help you fight your illness, this is not a one-size-fits-all approach. Everything here might not work for everyone, but I highly encourage you to examine them and see what you can apply to your life.

Another book on surviving terminal illness, *Remarkable Recovery*, by medical researcher Caryl Hirshberg and journalist Marc Barasch, shares hundreds of accounts of exceptional survivor stories. One unifying theme the authors found is the significant impact of spirituality, prayer, and community.[5]

Other researchers have documented the influence of prayer on the spontaneous remission of cancer. In 2004, a team in the Netherlands published a research paper entitled "Psychological changes preceding spontaneous remission of cancer." Psychological changes mentioned in their study included prayer, forgiveness, and spiritual experiences.[6]

Essentially, these findings suggest that healing from cancer starts from within the mind and the heart. It is an inside-out process that involves every part of you, including your spirit and soul. Negative emotions are not likely to benefit your healing and recovery. Letting them go and embracing positive emotions can help you cope with cancer symptoms, treatments, complications, and side effects. It can also help you heal. Cynthia's positivity and constant emotional support were most definitely a major part of my success.

As hard as it may be, I encourage you to do your best to surround yourself with positive and uplifting emotions. I highly recommend that hope, optimism, courage, joy, determination, and gratitude should be closely held principles that deserve your focused attention.

INTUITION

Intuition is seeing with the soul
   –Unknown

Another factor many authors of remission and recovery books have discussed is following your intuition. Intuition is defined as the ability to know something instinctively rather than by logic or reasoning. Many people have found that following their intuition about treatment options or lifestyle changes helped them fight cancer and reach remission.

One cancer survivor who shared his survival story and now works as a cancer coach is Glenn Sabin. Glenn was diagnosed with chronic lymphocytic leukemia—an aggressive form of blood cancer—and given six months to live. By following his intuition, allowing his own experience and results to guide his choices, he achieved and maintained remission. He also embraced daily exercise, a pescatarian diet, stress reduction, and dietary supplements.[7]

Glenn describes his story as one of "proactivity, perseverance and [resilience]."[8] And indeed, that is exactly the kind of attitude you need in the fight against cancer.

PURPOSE

Nothing will divert me from my purpose
   –Abraham Lincoln

Many survivors have also talked about how important it is to have a purpose in your life, a reason to live when it comes to surviving cancer. To survive a disease with such a high mortality rate, you need to have a reason for living—something that pushes you, inspires you, and makes you keep fighting.

Such a task, however, can be a daunting one, whether or not you are facing a potentially fatal illness. To get started on developing your purpose and reason to live, ask yourself some of the following questions:

- Why do you want to live?
- What is your purpose?
- What matters to you more than anything else in the world?
- What would you do anything for?
- What do you desperately want to witness, be, do, or have?

The answers to these questions can help you narrow in on the parts of your life you want to live for. Be sure to write these answers down, so you can continuously look over and review them to ensure your stay motivated.

Remember, fighting cancer is easier when you have a reason to live.

In his book about remarkable survivors, Jeff Rediger, MD, talks about ideologies or mindsets that are more likely to foreshadow a negative outcome. Summarized, they include:[9]

- Inflexibility associated with low self-esteem or a fixed worldview.
- Skepticism about self-help techniques or a limited ability to apply them.
- Meaning habitually sought outside the individual, from some external source.
- Strong, contrary views about the validity of spiritual ideas.

Conversely, the ideologies associated with a positive outcome were:

- A strong will to live.
- Changes in habits of thought and activity.
- Relaxation practices, meditation, mental imaging, cognitive monitoring.
- Becoming involved in a search for meaning in one's life

Finding meaning for your life from within is a crucial part of the process of surviving cancer. For some people, it might be the need to be there for their children, their parents, or any other loved one. This was most definitely the case for me. For others, it could be the desire to achieve milestones they had set and looked forward to for years. I found checking things off my bucket list to be an extremely rewarding experience. I still have some items on that list, and I continue to approach the task with fervour and a palpable sense of renewed purpose.

Whatever your purpose and reason to live is, find it, document it, and don't lose sight of it. The journey to remission is often long and filled with challenges. You need to focus on why you aren't giving up, why you aren't allowing cancer to kill your dreams and those of your loved ones.

You need to know what keeps you going, keeps you fighting, and keeps you strong. Find your reason for living and focus on it.

Appendix B

My Top Recommendations for Your Best Chances of Achieving Radical Remission

Throughout my journey with cancer, and especially now as I am in remission and living my best life, I've been asked what "things" helped me get through. Over the years, my answers have changed. After all, depending on where in my life I was at the time, I valued different things. However, now that I have had the time to reflect on my journey, I have narrowed my advice to five key points.

These are, in my opinion and with my extensive cancer experience, critical "must-haves" in your life to better your chances of surviving cancer and arriving at a thriving state of remission.

You Must Know Your Biomarkers

As discussed in Chapter 14, biomarkers are genetic codes held within your cells. They can be found in both healthy and unhealthy cells and hold important clues and information about your body and the disease you may be suffering from.

It is important to know the biomarkers for your cancer for several reasons. Cancer, as a disease, affects each person a little differently. Everyone's body and genes are slightly different. Similarly, cancer cells will also function within each body in slightly different ways. Some of these differences are negligible; however, other differences, even very small ones, can have a dramatic impact on the body. Your biomarkers carry information about how your cancer is growing and how your body is naturally reacting to the illness—both positively and negatively.

This can be a huge advantage in surviving the disease. These biomarkers can lend their information to help you decide which treatment to choose and how to change your lifestyle to give yourself the best chance possible to thrive after cancer.

You Must Use Technology to Your Advantage

In many ways, technology related to the advancements in the treatments of my cancer helped to keep it from growing. There is one specific piece of technology that gave me, perhaps, the most help and solace in my fight and journey: my mobile phone. Now that mobile phones can access the internet in nearly every context and situation, you have at your fingertips an endless supply of knowledge - some excellent and others, well, not so much.

Using our mobile phones, Cynthia and I were able to do our own research into my disease and bring novel ideas to my treatment team for consideration. We were able to find peer-reviewed articles about advancements in treatments and subsequently bring those articles to my appointments to have doctors further explain them to us. I was able to familiarize myself with some of the next steps of my journey to better prepare myself. I was also able to connect with other cancer sufferers and survivors to listen to their stories and draw advice from their experiences.

Such research helped us not only to find answers but to ask questions, as well. Through our research and exploration of cancer online, we kept on discovering questions that led to new information. We felt as if we were investigative journalists on the hunt for nuggets of key pieces of information. But this wasn't for a news article or a TV news piece. Indeed, this was to extend my life. The analogy to a journalist rings true here, as does the pressure to meet the "deadline."

Ultimately, our insatiable appetite for information and the positive reinforcement it provided gave us increasingly more confidence in my diagnosis and possible treatments.

An important note to highlight for patients with rare cancers: When researching, it will be difficult to locate peer-reviewed research journals. And if you're lucky enough to access them, a major source of additional information is found in the citations. All peer-reviewed journals are supported by previous or concurrent research. This means that if you look into the citations (footnotes) of a target journal, you will have likely tapped into a vein of new data. Keep doing that until you have amassed several good peer-reviewed journals for your type of cancer. Also, remember that research into rare cancers often contains reports that correspond to very few cancer patients. So the more research you do should translate into having access to more studies that may corroborate a particular treatment approach for your cancer type.

YOU MUST PRACTICE COMMUNICATION AND ASK THE QUESTIONS YOU WANT

Once you know what questions you want to ask, you must cultivate the courage to ask them. This is my third "must-have." To survive and keep your cancer at bay, you must be able to identify and ask the questions you need answers to and share your concerns.

For some, being surrounded by doctors, medical professionals, and even other cancer patients upon entering the cancer arena can be intimidating; it can feel like you do not have a voice. You are continuously told what the next steps are and what is going on in your body. It may even seem like your body and life are totally out of your control.

While your team of doctors will give you opportunities to ask any questions you have, you may not feel able to articulate them. You may even feel as though your questions are not good enough to be asked or that your questions are not rooted in science or on the same intellectual level as a cancer expert. But you are an expert. You are both an expert and an authority on the exceptionally important subject of your existence. And that gives you the right to exert your authority, within reason.

If you want to survive your illness, you must build the courage to ask those questions and claim your authority. The first step is knowing that those questions—any questions you may have—are good enough, valid, and justified. Second, asking your questions may give your doctors some insight into how you are handling the process and how your medical team can make your journey less challenging. They may help to make your treatment more effective. It is imperative to remember that the questions you ask can empower you in ways that can have a dramatic impact on your quest to survive.

I found that, especially when the fog of the illness began to set in, my developed communication skills helped me get what I needed throughout my journey. I want you to feel empowered to achieve a similar experience that leads you to the same outcome of remission and feeling empowered.

YOU MUST LOOK BEYOND CANCER

You may feel as though your life is out of your control - and in some respects, this may be true. Focusing on cancer all the time can bring about more emotional trauma than the cancer itself.

Through treatment, your body may be weakened in its attempt to repair itself, so your mind must be strong to help your body push through. To promote your emotional health, I encourage you to look at your life beyond cancer. Look at your hobbies or create new ones. Consider doing something that you always wanted to do. These will help keep your mind somewhat distracted from the battle going on within your body and help provide the motivation you need to keep moving forward.

There is also the important recommendation to not avoid making plans for the future. If your cancer is designated as terminal, you may fall into the trap of telling yourself something like:

"What good is planning for the future when I am terminally ill?"

Don't let yourself fall into this trap. I did at the beginning, and it wasn't good. It helped to support my initial negative thinking about my chances of survival. I wouldn't even buy a new shirt or replace underwear. I would tell myself, "Why would I spend 10 cents on something as trivial as those items if I'm going to die?" I remember when my passport needed to be renewed in 2017, and I was faced with the choice between renewing for 5 or 10 years. I decided on the 5-year option. But since then, I've benefited from much of the advice that I offer in this book. It's now 5 years later, and my passport needs to be renewed again. I think you can probably guess that my passport is now good til 2033, even if I'm not. But if I am, my goal is to follow my own advice and do my best to renew again in 2033.

No matter how bad the illness may be, there is always a chance of coming through the other end, alive and well; I am living proof of that. Making plans for your future can help you stay motivated to fight and to survive cancer.

For me, I learned how to play better backgammon online. At first, it was just for my own amusement, but once I found out there were competitions, I could not help myself from getting serious about it. I entered and planned to play in backgammon tournaments throughout my cancer journey; in fact, I still do now. Backgammon is one of the reasons I am thriving today.

YOU MUST FIND APPRECIATION

The last item on my list of must-haves is gratitude. It may be hard to find any reason to be grateful for your life or the people in your life when you are going through a horrific journey like cancer treatment.

However, finding appreciation and something to be grateful for is a key to living a thriving life after cancer. Whether it be your partner, a friend, your medical team, or another loved one, you must find gratitude for the people around you, as it will be another way for you to keep yourself motivated to get through your illness.

For my own cancer journey, I have many people and aspects to be grateful for. I had the support of a great family and group of friends who helped me through my fight. And while I may not have said it to them enough at the time, I sure do tell them how thankful I am now. There was one more person in my life that I am and will be forever grateful for, and that is my girlfriend, Cynthia. She was not only there for me through the worst parts of my fight, but she was also the one who actively fought for me and on my behalf when I was not able to—and when I wanted to give up.

People like Cynthia, and the rest of my family, are the ones you need to have in your corner during a fight like this. These are the kind of people you can find appreciation for. These are the kinds of people that will help you get through to the other side of your illness—and possibly on the other side of terminal where you can enjoy additional and precious time to live, love, laugh, and thrive.

I warmly invite you to please join me.

Appendix C

Recommended Resources

The Princess Margaret Cancer Centre

https://www.uhn.ca/PrincessMargaret

Part of Toronto's University Health Network, the Princess Margaret Cancer Centre is where my life was saved. They hold an extra special place in my heart and in the hearts of my family and friends. It's no surprise that The Princess Margaret was well-positioned to facilitate my life-saving therapy. As one of the top five cancer research centres in the world, it's the only 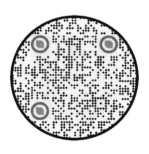 multi-disciplined treatment centre in Canada devoted solely to cancer care. Cancer is the only thing they "do," and I felt from day one that I was in very capable hands.

The Princess Margaret continues to be recognized internationally for important discoveries that have led to saving lives across the world. Their ground-breaking discoveries in the laboratory often lead to translational activity in clinical applications and trials. All this critical work is designed with one thing in mind: saving lives. They are a world leader in the areas of cancer stem cell research, image-guided therapeutics, and patient survivorship program development.

One of the cornerstones of sound scientific research is an institution's credibility and reputation in its research activity. Each year, The Princess Margaret publishes more than one thousand original peer-reviewed publications, contributing to the global effort to understand cancer and offer better treatments for patients. They are ranked second in the world for research papers cited in high-impact oncology journals and fifth for highly cited research papers.

The Princess Margaret Cancer Foundation

https://thepmcf.ca/

Because two in five Canadians will be diagnosed with cancer in their lifetime, the Princess Margaret Cancer Foundation passionately engages the community to raise crucial funds, helping drive world-class cancer research forward and set new standards of care.

With a laser-focused vision to *Conquer Cancer In Our Lifetime,* their mission is to enable *Future Care Now* by raising funds that accelerate cancer research, education, and clinical care benefitting patients at Princess Margaret Cancer Centre—across Canada and around the world.

The Princess Margaret Cancer Foundation achieves much of their goals with recurring and very popular fundraising events such as the Princess Margaret Home Lottery, Enbridge® Ride to Conquer Cancer®, Walk to Conquer Cancer, Journey to Conquer Cancer, and many others. Please scan this QR code and consider donating to this very worthy cause that is near and dear to me.

Access to Comprehensive Genomic Profiling (ACGP)

https://accesstocgp.com/

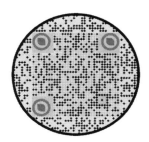

Access to Comprehensive Genomic Profiling (ACGP) aims to raise awareness about comprehensive genomic profiling (CGP) for advanced cancer patients. The coalition seeks to educate stakeholders about the value of CGP tests in all tumour types, to assure appropriate use in the patient journey, to inform medical management and improve clinical outcomes.

ACGP is dedicated to sharing the clinical utility and economic value of CGP with healthcare stakeholders with the view of increasing access to this innovative technology, particularly in the United States. A lot of the information found at their website will apply to most cancer patients who are considering NGS assessment, regardless of where they live. They have some great FAQ's and they identify the companies within their membership that can help you discover the best treatment for your cancer.

CLINICALTRIALS.GOV

https://www.clinicaltrials.gov/

Clinical trials are real-time experiments with human beings using novel drugs that may be of tremendous value. They help doctors find better treatments for cancers and other diseases, and they can help you gain access to new or experimental therapies that might help you achieve remission. When there seems to be no hope left, many individuals will enter clinical 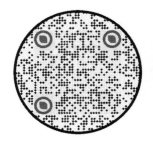 trials not only to help themselves survive their own cancer but help add to the growing body of cancer research with the view of helping others.

The first step to joining a clinical trial is to research it and discuss it with your doctor. With a little practice, you can search for clinical trials on your own. The websites are country-specific; however, many clinical trials have cross-over into other jurisdictions, thereby sometimes allowing patients to enrol from other countries. Some American clinical trials have satellite health centres that include clinical settings in Canada and other countries. Just be sure to look at credible websites; do not simply pick the first one you find.

One of the most popular clinical trial websites that you may want to look into is ClinicalTrials.gov from the American National Institute of Health's National Library of Medicine. It's an incredibly extensive database of privately and publicly funded clinical studies conducted around the world. It is very possible that the keys to a longer life could be found within this database.

The National Cancer Institute Clinical Trials Checklist

**www.cancer.gov/about-cancer/treatment/clinical-trials/search/
trial-guide/detailschecklist.pdf**

All clinical trials have a protocol in which they spell out the criteria for joining. You will need to check if you meet the eligibility criteria before contacting the investigators. This National Cancer Institute checklist helps you gather your information for easy access during screening.

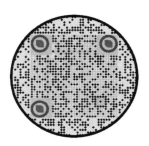

Wellspring Cancer Support

https://wellspring.ca

In Canada, a cancer support centre called Wellspring is available at no charge to help cancer patients, caregivers, and family members elevate their quality of life through a strengthened mind and body.

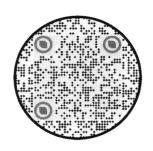

I was lucky to have participated in a 12-week-long young adult group of eight people led by Dr. Mavis Himes, a highly regarded clinical psychologist and psychoanalyst and author of two books. I engaged deeply in our weekly sessions and put much of what we learned into daily practice. I can't recommend enough that those who are fighting or have fought cancer get involved with a support group.

TargetCancer Foundation and TRACK

https://www.targetcancerfoundation.org

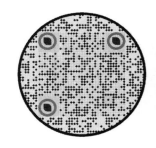

TargetCancer Foundation is a beacon of hope for patients and families affected by rare cancers. Their mission is to promote the development of lifesaving treatment protocols for rare cancers. They achieve this by directly supporting initiatives at the forefront of cancer treatment through funding innovative research, fostering collaborations, and raising awareness among scientists, clinicians, and patients.

One of the key challenges with rare cancers is that many patients are excluded from clinical trials. To address this, TargetCancer Foundation has expanded its impact through a prospective clinical trial called TCF-001 TRACK (Target Rare Cancer Knowledge) which seeks to enrol 400 patients with rare cancers or cancer of unknown primary.

TRACK provides participating rare cancer patients and their physicians with personalized, actionable information to potentially inform treatment, as well as recommendations from an expert panel of rare cancer clinicians and scientists. At the same time, TRACK generates critical genomic data to drive a better understanding of often overlooked rare cancers. Through an innovative remote consenting process, patients can fully consent and enrol in the TRACK study from their home, without travelling to a clinical trial site.

If you or a loved one are facing a rare cancer, you would be wise to consider reaching out to TargetCancer Foundation. At the time of the publication of this book, TRACK can only enrol patients from the United States; however, by the time you are reading this, those guidelines may have changed—or there could be another clinical trial, or they may have entered into agreements with partners in Canada or other countries.

Regardless, TargetCancer Foundation is a light that shines further and brighter each day for those with rare cancers.

United States Backgammon Federation

https://usbgf.org/

Since the impossible backgammon win that made it all "click" for me, I have gathered the courage to place myself in competitive tournament play within the United States Backgammon Federation, going up against some of the best players in the world. Despite my abysmal odds and the amateur status that I entered the tournament with, I have won four tournaments and placed second in several others.

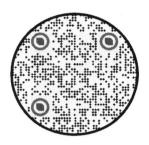

More important than winning money in these tournaments or seeing my name published, is that the message of continued survival despite horrible odds seems to be persisting for me. Even if it seems that you don't have a chance to survive, think again, because you do. Fight *hard*, make wise decisions, and never give up hope.

It's utterly amazing that, of all things, it was my love for the game of backgammon and my competitive nature that opened the door to a deep level of understanding I never knew existed. Playing the game of backgammon showed me just how real the possibility of success is when you play the game to win. So, I encourage you to go find your own door. It's there—all you have to do is find it, open it, and walk through.

Acknowledgments

Ethan and Hila: In my darkest days, you were the brightest lights that helped guide me through to the other side. And now, your promising lives prevent me from giving up so we can live another day together. My hope is that this book will serve as a permanent reminder of the love we showered on each other and the guidance I was lucky enough to offer you. Allow my life and the values I shared to continually guide you to be wholesome and compassionate people to yourselves and to others. I will always be your biggest supporter because of the special place you allow me to occupy in your hearts.

Mom & Dad: Thank you for always being my two unwavering pillars of support and for offering unyielding love and concern. The strength and resilience you've shown me through impossible circumstances was the one life lesson that helped me to be strong for myself, when I needed it most.

Cynthia: Our hearts were eternally bound together from the day we met. Words don't exist to convey the love and gratitude I have for you. What you have done for me, for us, and for our families is the most heroic thing I have ever seen or experienced. I am awe-struck by you and your instinctive desire to continuously offer support in the most loving ways. I'm the luckiest person to have you!

Elena and Hayden: Thank you for supporting your mom and for understanding my need to come to terms with my illness before I was able to fully let you in.

My Family: Thank you for your love and support.

Dr. Madeline Li: Thank you for not giving up on me and my family and for always believing that we could do great work together. You turned me around 180 degrees and sent me off to live the life I needed to live. It's clear that you love your work, and I'm profoundly grateful to have been a beneficiary of your diagnostic skills and professional support.

The Princess Margaret Cancer Centre: Thank you for providing me with exemplary care and being open to my self-advocacy. Believing that a novel approach to my treatment could extend my life was a pivotal decision for my survival. I hope that the success I've enjoyed will help shape the care at PMH for other patients with rare cancers.

The Princess Margaret Cancer Foundation: Thank you for your unrelenting efforts and community involvement to deliver best-in-class cancer research for Ontario, Canada, and the international community. I fully support and believe in your mission that we could end cancer in our lifetime.

Foundation Medicine: Thank you for your contribution to the growing application of comprehensive genomic profiling in cancer care and its immeasurable impact on patient lives. Without your continued advancements and discoveries at the bench, there would be little in the way to translate to the bedside. Please keep pushing forward.

TargetCancer Foundation: Thank you for elevating the importance of rare cancer research. I firmly believe that the discoveries that follow from your ongoing efforts will have an incredible impact on the greater cancer community. Perhaps the key to a cure will be found within a rare cancer discovery. May Paul's memory be a blessing.

Steve Pottins: Your friendship and professional guidance throughout the last 18 years has been one of the most important impacts on my various journeys. Thank you.

Mark & Lila: Thank you for constantly offering your kindness and love even when I wasn't able to properly receive it.

Marni Appel: Thank you for stepping up in the most unexpected ways. No more soup please, ever!

My friends: Thank you for your support and for understanding that I needed my space to process difficult emotions. Your persistence is a testament to our friendship.

Dr. Nsisong Asanga: In addition to your other valued suggestions, your assistance on the epidemiology aspects for this book have proved invaluable. Thank you.

Dr. Mavis Himes: Working closely together as co-facilitators was an absolute honour. With your professional guidance, we helped many young adults with cancer have an easier journey.

USBGF: Thank you for warmly including this Canadian into your American BG family.

Rachel Schultz: Thank you for being a tireless editing partner extraordinaire.

References

Introduction

1. "WHO Report on Cancer: Setting Priorities, Investing Wisely and Providing Care for All." World Health Organization. February 3, 2020. https://www.who.int/publications-detail-redirect/who-report-on-cancer-setting-priorities-investing-wisely-and-providing-care-for-all.
2. "Depression (PDQ®)–Health Professional Version." National Cancer Institute. Last updated March 4, 2022. https://www.cancer.gov/about-cancer/coping/feelings/depression-hp-pdq.
3. Henley, S. Jane, Elizabeth M. Ward, Susan Scott, Jiemin Ma, Robert N. Anderson, Albert U. Firth, Cheryll C. Thomas, et al. "Annual Report to the Nation on the Status of Cancer, Part I: National Cancer Statistics." *Cancer* 126, no. 10 (2020): 2225–49. https://doi.org/10.1002/cncr.32802.

4. Understanding Cancer

1. "Cancer Statistics at a Glance." Canadian Cancer Society. Accessed March 14, 2022. https://cancer.ca/en/research/cancer-statistics/cancer-statistics-at-a-glance.
2. "What is Cancer?" Cancer.net. October 4, 2019. https://www.cancer.net/navigating-cancer-care/cancer-basics/what-c%C3%A1ncer.
3. ibid.

9. Helpless Without a Cause

1. Brose, Marcia S., Thomas C. Smyrk, Barbara Weber, and Henry T. Lynch. "Genetic Basis of Cancer Syndromes." *Holland-Frei Cancer Medicine.* 6th edition. Hamilton, ON: BC Decker, 2003. https://www.ncbi.nlm.nih.gov/books/NBK12959/.
2. Reif, Arnold E. "The Causes of Cancer: While Some Cancers Are Genetically Fated to Appear, Most Have Now Been Traced to Environmental Factors." *American Scientist* 69, no. 4 (1981): 437–47. http://www.jstor.org/stable/27850536.
3. IARC Working Group on the Evaluation of Carcinogenic Risks to Humans. "Ionizing Radiation, Part 1: X- and Gamma (γ)-Radiation, and Neutrons." Lyon, FR: International Agency for Research on Cancer, 2000. (*IARC Monographs on the Evaluation of Carcinogenic Risks to Humans*, no. 75.) https://www.ncbi.nlm.nih.gov/books/NBK401331/.
4. Pöschl, G., H. K. Seitz. "Alcohol and Cancer." *Alcohol and Alcoholism* 39, no. 3 (2004): 155–65. https://doi.org/10.1093/alcalc/agh057.

5. Donaldson, Michael S. "Nutrition and Cancer: A Review of the Evidence for an Anti-Cancer Diet." *Nutrition Journal* 3, no. 1 (2004). https://doi.org/10.1186/1475-2891-3-19.

6. Avgerinos, Konstantinos I., Nikolaos Spyrou, Christos S. Mantzoros, and Maria Dalamaga. "Obesity and Cancer Risk: Emerging Biological Mechanisms and Perspectives." *Metabolism* 92 (2019): 121–35. https://doi.org/10.1016/j.metabol.2018.11.001.

7. English, Dallas R., Bruce K. Armstrong, Anne Kricker, and Claire Fleming. *Cancer Causes and Control* 8, no. 3 (1997): 271–83. https://doi.org/10.1023/a:1018440801577.

8. Reznikov, A. "Hormonal Impact on Tumor Growth and Progression." *Experimental Oncology* 37, no. 3 (2015): 162-72. PMID: 26422099.

9. Ji, Yongjia, and Hongzhou Lu. "Malignancies in HIV-Infected and AIDS Patients." *Advances in Experimental Medicine and Biology*, 2017, 167–79. https://doi.org/10.1007/978-981-10-5765-6_10.

10. Pawelec, Graham. "Immunosenescence and Cancer." *Biogerontology* 18, no. 4 (2017): 717–21. https://doi.org/10.1007/s10522-017-9682-z.

11. Murata, Mariko. "Inflammation and Cancer." *Environmental Health and Preventive Medicine* 23, no. 1 (2018). https://doi.org/10.1186/s12199-018-0740-1.

12. Oh, Jin-Kyoung, and Elisabete Weiderpass. "Infection and Cancer: Global Distribution and Burden of Diseases." *Annals of Global Health* 80, no. 5 (2014): 384. https://doi.org/10.1016/j.aogh.2014.09.013.

12. Understanding Cancer Staging

1. "Staging Cancer." Canadian Cancer Society. Accessed March 14, 2022. https://cancer.ca/en/cancer-information/what-is-cancer/stage-and-grade/staging.

2. Peters, M.V. "A Study of Survivals in Hodgkin's Disease Treated Radiologically." *American Journal of Roentgenology Radium Therapy and Nuclear Medicine* 101, no. 2 (1967): 492. http://doi.org/10.2214/ajr.101.2.492.

3. Rosenberg, S.A., M. Boiron, V. T. DeVita, et al. "Report of the Committee on Hodgkin's Disease Staging Procedures." *Cancer Research* 31, no. 11 (1971): 1862-3. PMID: 5121695.

4. Carbone, P.P., H.S. Kaplan, K. Musshoff, D.W. Smithers, M. Tubiana. (November 1971). "Report of the Committee on Hodgkin's Disease Staging Classification." *Cancer Research* 31, no. 11 (1971): 1860-1. PMID: 5121694.

5. Mauch, Peter M., James O. Armitage, Volker Diehl, Richard T. Hoppe, Lawrence M. Weiss. *Hodgkin's Disease*. Philadelphia: Lippincott Williams & Wilkins, 1999, 223–28. ISBN 978-0-7817-1502-7.

6. Cheson, Bruce D., Richard I. Fisher, Sally F. Barrington, Franco Cavalli, et al. "Recommendations for Initial Evaluation, Staging, and Response Assessment of Hodgkin and Non-Hodgkin Lymphoma: the Lugano Classification." *Journal of Clinical Oncology* 32, no. 27 (2014): 3059-68. PMID: 25113753.

7. "Stages of Hodgkin Lymphoma." Cancer Research UK. Last updated September 22, 2020. https://www.cancerresearchuk.org/about-cancer/hodgkin-lymphoma/stages.

13. My Treatment Choice and Motivation

1. Calasibetta, Charlotte Mankey. *Fairchild's Dictionary of Fashion*. 2nd ed. New York: Fairchild Publications, 1988, 363–64. ISBN: 1-56367-235-9.

14. Understanding Cancer Treatments

1. Patel, Parth, and Chris Thomas. "Building Back Cancer Services in England." Institute for Public Policy Research, September 2021. https://www.ippr.org/files/2021-09/building-back-cancer-services.pdf.
2. Malagón, Talía, Jean H. Yong, Parker Tope, Wilson H. Miller, and Eduardo L. Franco. "Predicted Long-Term Impact of Covid-19 Pandemic-Related Care Delays on Cancer Mortality in Canada." *International Journal of Cancer* 150, no. 8 (2021): 1244–54. https://doi.org/10.1002/ijc.33884.
3. "Cancer Treatment Types." Canadian Cancer Society. Accessed March 14, 2022. https://cancer.ca/en/treatments/treatment-types.
4. ibid.
5. ibid.
6. "What is Immunotherapy?" Cancer Research Institute. Accessed March 14, 2022. https://www.cancerresearch.org/en-us/immunotherapy/what-is-immunotherapy.
7. "Stem Cell Transplantation for Treating Cancer." Institute for Quality and Efficiency in Health Care. Last updated December 30, 2016. https://www.ncbi.nlm.nih.gov/books/NBK401241/.
8. "Understanding Targeted Therapy." Cancer.net. Accessed March 14, 2022. https://www.cancer.net/navigating-cancer-care/how-cancer-treated/personalized-and-targeted-therapies/understanding-targeted-therapy.
9. "Biomarker Testing for Cancer Treatment." National Cancer Institute. Last updated December 14, 2021. https://www.cancer.gov/about-cancer/treatment/types/biomarker-testing-cancer-treatment.
10. Kamps, Rick, Rita Brandão, Bianca Bosch, Aimee Paulussen, Sofia Xanthoulea, Marinus Blok, and Andrea Romano. "Next-Generation Sequencing in Oncology: Genetic Diagnosis, Risk Prediction and Cancer Classification." *International Journal of Molecular Sciences* 18, no. 2 (2017): 308. https://doi.org/10.3390/ijms18020308.
11. McKenzie, Andrew J., Holli H. Dilks, Suzanne F. Jones, and Howard Burris. "Should next-Generation Sequencing Tests Be Performed on All Cancer Patients?" *Expert Review of Molecular Diagnostics* 19, no. 2 (2019): 89–93. https://doi.org/10.1080/14737159.2019.1564043.
12. "Access to Comprehensive Genomic Profiling." ACGP.com. Accessed March 14, 2022. https://accesstocgp.com/.
13. "CAR T Cell: Engineering Patient's Cells to Treat their Cancers." National Cancer Institute. Accessed March 14, 2022. https://www.cancer.gov/about-cancer/treatment/research/car-t-cells.
14. "Top 10 Most Promising Cancer Treatments." Best Medical Degrees. Accessed March 14, 2022. https://www.bestmedicaldegrees.com/experimental-cancer-treatments.
15. Robey, Ian F., and Natasha K. Martin. "Bicarbonate and Dichloroacetate: Evaluating PH Altering Therapies in a Mouse Model for Metastatic Breast Cancer." *BMC Cancer*

11, no. 1 (2011). https://doi.org/10.1186/1471-2407-11-235.

16. Nam, Ju-Suk, Ashish Sharma, Lich Nguyen, Chiranjib Chakraborty, Garima Sharma, and Sang-Soo Lee. "Application of Bioactive Quercetin in Oncotherapy: From Nutrition to Nanomedicine." *Molecules* 21, no. 1 (2016): 108. https://doi.org/10.3390/molecules21010108.

17. "Opdivo-Yervoy Combination Approved for Melanoma—First Combination-Immunotherapy Regimen for Cancer." *Oncology Times* 37, no. 21 (2015): 39. https://doi.org/10.1097/01.cot.0000473604.35674.ee.

18. Postow, Michael A., Jason Chesney, Anna C. Pavlick, Caroline Robert, Kenneth Grossmann, David McDermott, Gerald P. Linette, et al. "Nivolumab and Ipilimumab versus Ipilimumab in Untreated Melanoma." New England Journal of Medicine 372, no. 21 (2015): 2006–17. https://doi.org/10.1056/nejmoa1414428.

19. Shoushtari, Alexander N., Claire F. Friedman, Pedram Navid-Azarbaijani, Michael A. Postow, Margaret K. Callahan, Parisa Momtaz, Katherine S. Panageas, Jedd D. Wolchok, and Paul B. Chapman. "Measuring Toxic Effects and Time to Treatment Failure for Nivolumab plus Ipilimumab in Melanoma." *JAMA Oncology* 4, no. 1 (2018): 98. https://doi.org/10.1001/jamaoncol.2017.2391.

20. McCarthy, Edward F. "The Toxins of William B. Coley and The Treatment of Bone and Soft-Tissue Sarcomas." Iowa Orthopedic Journal 26 (2006): 154-8. PMID: 16789469.

21. "Top 10 Most Promising Cancer Treatments." Best Medical Degrees. Accessed March 14, 2022. https://www.bestmedicaldegrees.com/experimental-cancer-treatments/.

22. Robey, Ian F, and Natasha K Martin. "Bicarbonate and Dichloroacetate: Evaluating Ph Altering Therapies in a Mouse Model for Metastatic Breast Cancer." *BMC Cancer* 11, no. 1 (2011). https://doi.org/10.1186/1471-2407-11-235.

23. Nam, Ju-Suk, Ashish Sharma, Lich Nguyen, Chiranjib Chakraborty, Garima Sharma, and Sang-Soo Lee. "Application of Bioactive Quercetin in Oncotherapy: From Nutrition to Nanomedicine." *Molecules* 21, no. 1 (2016): 108. https://doi.org/10.3390/molecules21010108.

24. ibid.

21. TREATING A RARE CANCER

1. "Rare Cancer." NCI Dictionary of Cancer Terms. Accessed March 14, 2022. https://www.cancer.gov/publications/dictionaries/cancer-terms/def/rare-cancer.

2. "Appendix B: Metadata: Surveillance, Epidemiology, and End Results (SEER) Program." Environmental Protection Agency. *America's Children and the Environment*. 3rd ed. October 2019. https://www.epa.gov/sites/default/files/2015-06/documents/aceappendixb_surveillanceepidemiologyandendresults.pdf.

3. "What is a Rare Cancer?" Cancer Research UK. Last updated August 23, 2019. https://www.cancerresearchuk.org/about-cancer/rare-cancers/what-rare-cancers-are.

4. "Developing Products for Rare Diseases & Conditions." U.S. Food & Drug Administration. Accessed March 14, 2022. https://www.fda.gov/industry/developing-products-rare-diseases-conditions.

5. "FY 2018 Research Funding by Cancer Type." National Cancer Institute. Accessed March 14, 2022. https://fundedresearch.cancer.gov/nciportfolio/search/funded?

fy=PUB2018&type=site.

24. Understanding Remission

1. "Remission." NCI Dictionary of Cancer Terms. Accessed March 14, 2022. https://www.cancer.gov/publications/dictionaries/cancer-terms/def/remission.
2. Chang, W. Y. "Complete Spontaneous Regression of Cancer: Four Case Reports, Review of Literature, and Discussion of Possible Mechanisms Involved." *Hawaii Medical Journal* 59, no. 10 (2000): 379-87. PMID: 11789163.
3. Turner, Kelly A. *Radical Remission: Surviving Cancer Against All Odds.* New York, NY: HarperOne, 2015.
4. "Five-Year Survival Rate." NCI Dictionary of Cancer Terms. Accessed March 14, 2022. https://www.cancer.gov/publications/dictionaries/cancer-terms/def/five-year-survival-rate.

Appendix A

1. Lăcătuşu, Cristina-Mihaela, Elena-Daniela Grigorescu, Mariana Floria, Alina Onofriescu, and Bogdan-Mircea Mihai. "The Mediterranean Diet: From an Environment-Driven Food Culture to an Emerging Medical Prescription." International Journal of Environmental Research and Public Health 16, no. 6 (2019): 942. https://doi.org/10.3390/ijerph16060942.
2. Gunnars, Kris. "How Much Water Should You Drink Per Day?" Healthline. Last updated November 5, 2020. https://www.healthline.com/nutrition/how-much-water-should-you-drink-per-day.
3. Rajarajeswaran, P, and R Vishnupriya. "Exercise in Cancer." Indian Journal of Medical and Paediatric Oncology 30, no. 02 (2009): 61–70. https://doi.org/10.4103/0971-5851.60050.
4. Turner, Kelly A. *Radical Remission: Surviving Cancer Against All Odds.* New York, NY: HarperOne, 2015.
5. Hirshberg, Caryle and Marc Ian Barasch. *Remarkable Recovery: What Extraordinary Healings Tells Us About Getting Well and Staying Well.* 1st ed. Diane Pub Co, 1999. ISBN: 978-0788161742.
6. Schilder, Johannes N., Marco J. de Vries, Karl Goodkin, and Mike Antoni. "Psychological Changes Preceding Spontaneous Remission of Cancer." *Clinical Case Studies* 3, no. 4 (2004): 288–312. https://doi.org/10.1177/1534650103259631.
7. Sabin, Glenn. *N of 1: One Man's Harvard-Documented Remission of Incurable Cancer Using Only Natural Methods.* 1st ed. Fon Press, 2016. ISBN: 978-0997548204.
8. ibid.
9. Rediger, Jeffrey. *Cured: Strengthen Your Immune System and Heal Your Life.* 1st ed. Flatiron Books, February 2, 2021. ISBN: 978-1250193216.